A HANDBOOK
FOR CORRECTIONAL
PSYCHOLOGISTS

ABOUT THE AUTHOR

Kevin M. Correia, Ph.D. is a clinical psychologist in both public and private practice. He currently serves as the Chief Psychologist at the Federal Correctional Complex in Beaumont, Texas. He maintains a private practice in Beaumont, Texas, focused on individual and family therapy and assessment. He is a graduate of Auburn University with primary interests in the area of personality assessment, developmental psychology and correctional treatment programs.

Second Edition

A HANDBOOK FOR CORRECTIONAL PSYCHOLOGISTS

Guidance for the Prison Practitioner

By

KEVIN M. CORREIA, PH.D.

Federal Correctional Complex
Beaumont, Texas

CHARLES C THOMAS • PUBLISHER, LTD.
Springfield • Illinois • U.S.A.

Published and Distributed Throughout the World by

CHARLES C THOMAS • PUBLISHER, LTD.
2600 South First Street
Springfield, Illinois 62704

© 2009 by CHARLES C THOMAS • PUBLISHER, LTD.

ISBN 978-0-398-07849-2 (hard)
ISBN 978-0-398-07850-8 (paper)

Library of Congress Catalog Card Number: 2008041630

With THOMAS BOOKS *careful attention is given to all details of manufacturing
and design. It is the Publisher's desire to present books that are satisfactory as to their
physical qualities and artistic possibilities and appropriate for their particular use.*
THOMAS BOOKS *will be true to those laws of quality that assure a good name
and good will.*

Printed in the United States of America
LAH-R-3

Library of Congress Cataloging-in-Publication Data

Correia, Kevin M.
  A handbook for correctional psychologists : guidance for the prison practitioner / by
Kevin M. Correia.
     p. cm.
  Includes bibliographical references and index.
  ISBN 978-0-398-07849-2 (hard) -- ISBN 978-0-398-07850-8 (pbk.)
   1.   Prison psychologists--Handbooks, manuals, etc. 2.   Prison psychology--
Handbooks, manuals, etc. I. Title.

  HV6089.C67 2009
  365'.6672--dc22

                                                             2008041630

PREFACE

Correctional psychology is an area of specialization that has recently enjoyed explosive growth along with the burgeoning United States prison population and renewed interest in providing correctional rehabilitation programs that reduce inmate recidivism. *A Handbook for Correctional Psychologists* provides an overview of empirical findings and practices of the field. It serves as an introduction to basic principles of correctional psychology for the psychologist-practitioner working within, or contemplating working within, a correctional setting. It focuses specifically on the psychologist's role within a correctional institutional setting and clarifies the differences in working with inmates and correctional staff from populations more commonly encountered by those working in the field of psychology. It summarizes the state of current relevant research and offers practical advice and examples for successfully transitioning into this environment. Topics covered include trends in correctional psychology, unique aspects of the correctional work environment, the many roles and opportunities of the correctional psychologist, establishing successful relationships with correctional staff and inmates, and assessing malingering through the use of interviewing or psychometric evaluation. This book serves as a reference for those within the field and an investigative tool for those contemplating entering this field so that they may make a more informed decision as to whether such work would be a good fit for them. The book is an excellent way of exposing graduate students to the applied aspects of psychology and/or criminal justice at the graduate level.

DISCLAIMER

The views expressed in this article represent those of the author and do not necessarily reflect those of the Federal Bureau of Prisons or the U.S. Department of Justice.

CONTENTS

A HANDBOOK
FOR CORRECTIONAL
PSYCHOLOGISTS

Chapter 1

INTRODUCTION

THIS AUTHOR HAS THE RECOLLECTION of attending the funeral of a family member during his days as a graduate student when he was approached by a distant relative he had not seen in several years. She was a particularly outgoing individual and immediately upon approaching the author enveloped him in a warm interaction designed to reconnect after such a long time. After a matter of only a couple of minutes she asked the fateful question of what endeavors the author was currently involved with. Upon informing her of his alliance with the field of clinical psychology the author noticed a sea-change in her demeanor. The friendly warm smile was replaced with an apprehensive stare and a stiffening movement coursed through her entire body. She suddenly remembered some forgotten responsibility elsewhere, excused herself too politely and disappeared among the various funeral attendees.

I learned then that people have many different reactions to learning that one is a psychologist, and frankly, the negative and apprehensive reactions seem to greatly outnumber the positive and warm ones. Perhaps some believe that psychologists possess mystical powers of being able to peer through others protective veneer and isolate the deviant aspect of their being without there being any way of stopping it. Undoubtedly, much of the reaction comes from an insecurity about themselves and a basic misperception about psychologists in general. Certainly they do not realize most psychologists lack of personal concern into the intrapsychic motivations of casual acquaintances, friends and family, although I must admit when one virtually runs away screaming at the first indication of my chosen profession that I cannot help but make mental notations regarding their abnormal behavior. With experience I came to appreciate people like my relative who took flight from my powers. After all, this is far preferable to others who assume that psychologists want to know everything about them and quickly begin revealing intimate details of their lives in hopes that a few minutes with a psychologist will allow them to uncover what has ailed them for so many years or perhaps unlock the key to their spouse's or child's pathology.

It is tempting to believe that perhaps this was why professionals unite into organizations devoted to their chosen field. Do not doctors get solicitations for medical advice from casual acquaintances? Do not lawyers receive masked or outright requests for legal advice from virtual strangers? And how about the plumber down the street who never seemed to get around to answering the question about why my toilet makes that ungodly noise? All right, so perhaps this phenomena is not so unusual. However, I noticed that something happened to my own colleagues when I decided to apply my skills to the field of corrections. I was accepted as a psychologist easily enough. But when mention of my work site entered the conversation I realized I had developed within my personal arsenal another way of distancing myself from others. All I had to do was divulge that I practiced within the confines of a prison. I now had a way of distancing myself from my colleagues and a choice of two alternatives of how to stop conversations with those outside the field. After all, laypeople respond no more affectionately to revelations that one works within a prison than they do to news that you are a psychologist. Either piece of information can easily result in raised eyebrows, a heightened stare and a tightening of the lips. All of this brings us to the purpose of the present publication. If psychologists are misunderstood, then correctional psychologists are doubly so.

SEPARATING FACT FROM FICTION: THE TRUTH ABOUT WORKING IN A CORRECTIONAL ENVIRONMENT

The idea of working as a psychologist in a correctional setting is one full of ideas about dealing with maniacal lunatics, extremely violent individuals, reforming those most in need of assistance, and other somewhat naive assumptions of what it must be like. The truth of the matter is that while there may be some substance to each of these conceptions, our imaginations tend to run wild and take them to extremes that have no basis in reality. It is surprising that given the number of psychologists that currently work full or part-time in correctional settings that there is very little information as to what they do in these environments and how they go about it. There are few training programs that provide much information, if any, on this area of specialization such that when it comes time to find gainful employment (yes, there is an end to graduate school) the only information to go on when considering possible positions in the correctional field are these vague ideas, which emanate more from movies than reality. Most graduate programs spend more time discussing the behavior of rodents than prison inmates. In the present environment of government cutbacks, along with modern realizations that rats are not as neurotic as initially believed (nor very well insured), finding gainful employment treating such rodents is becoming more difficult. Thus, perhaps our training programs are doing us some disservice.

The realities of working in a prison environment are quite different than most people imagine. It is both better and worse than most people might think. Hopefully as you read through the following chapters this last statement will make sense and you will finish with a better idea of what correctional psychologists do and/or have some ideas/clarifications of how to most effectively go about your job if you have already taken the plunge and accepted a position in the field. Much of the information contained in this book are data that I found myself discovering, needing, or at least wanting, as I launched into the field of correctional psychology. In learning and looking for the information I was surprised that there existed no single general source of such knowledge, so that I was made to gather it from a motley collection of often difficult to find journal articles and books. Part of the motivation for the present publication, then, is to organize the data thus collected and provide a single cohesive source of materials for other correctional psychologists.

The goal of the ensuing chapters, then, is to provide a general introduction and overview to what correctional psychologists do, the differences one encounters in doing clinical work in a correctional setting, some prescriptions on successfully interacting with both inmates and correctional staff, and some considerations one may wish to contemplate to accurately discern if working in the correctional field is appropriate for the reader. A general view of the current and possible future status of psychologists working in the field, as well as the general state of the correctional field itself is presented. Additionally, some specific attention is given to the issues of detecting malingering and deception amongst inmates, because there is more often sufficient motivation for clients in this setting to attempt to feign mental illness. Additionally, the field has progressed fairly well in methods of distinguishing true from feigned mental illness through investigative research, but has sometimes not been as successful in disseminating the results to psychologists in the field. The present book explores this issue from both an interviewing and a psychometric approach. Finally, because these very same issues often threaten to arise in legal proceedings, some discussion is presented about proper approaches and methods for being comfortable in the role of expert witness in criminal proceedings.

This book is not meant to be an authoritative source of knowledge, but strives to provide a basic resource from which any more detailed searches can be launched. Much of the writing herein also represents my personal views and is based on my personal experiences and interactions with others in the field. There is no representation made as to its representing the Federal Bureau of Prisons to which the author is currently employed or any other public or private entity. I do not profess to have found the single most effective way of performing the duties of a correctional psychologist, but hope through the dissemination of this book to stimulate others in the field to develop a more organized cognitive framework for the work they do and the environment in which it occurs. Additionally, it is my hope that this manual will be utilized as an investigative tool for those contemplating entering this field so that they may make a more informed decision as to whether it provides a good fit for them. Finally, perhaps some enlightened members of the academic establishment will view this manual and others like it as a way of exposing graduate students to the applied aspects of our field prior to their graduation. As for how to deal with those prickly responses of others first learning of your chosen profession: tell them you are a janitor at an elementary school and then analyze the hell out of them!

GROWTH OF CORRECTIONS IN THE UNITED STATES

In recent years there has been a burgeoning growth in the number of prisons and prisoners in the United States fueled by an increasingly aggressive enforcement and prosecution of drug and other crimes, a trend toward increasing the length of sentences served by convicted offenders, a push to force convicted offenders to serve a greater percentage of their assigned sentences, an end or move away from paroling offenders and an increasing popularity of career offender laws, which further lengthen sentences of repeat offenders.

From 1990 to 1999 the rate of prison and jail incarceration jumped from 458 per 100,000 U.S. residents to 682 per 100,000 (U.S. Department of Justice, 2000). By 2005, the United States reached an incarceration rate of 737 persons per 100,000 US residents. In 2005, about 1 out of every 136 U.S. residents was incarcerated either in prison or jail (Harrison & Beck, 2006). The United States has 5 percent of the world's population and 25 percent of the world's incarcerated population (Bureau of Justice Statistics, 2007).

The U.S. incarcerated population showed an average increase of 5.8 percent from 1990 to 1999 (U.S. Department of Justice, 2000). Federal Prison populations showed an average annual increase of 8.5 percent during the same period. From 1990 to 1997 the United States state prison population of sentenced inmates increased from 708,393 to 1,131,581 (Gilliard & Beck, 1998). During these years the Nation's prison inmate population grew more than 60 percent. At midyear 2007, the Nation's prisons and jails incarcerated 2,299,116 persons (Bureau of Justice Statistics, 2006). The rate of growth has been unprecedented and translates into the equivalent of an additional 1,610 more prisoners every week in the period 1990–1999 (U.S. Department of Justice, 2000). Other than an increase in drug education and drug treatment programs, this population explosion has not generally been accompanied by corresponding growth in rehabilitative programs.

In recent years, budget pressures created by increasingly short-sighted government policies and the incredible cost to the Federal government of engaging in costs associated with various military excursions has led to a somewhat disturbing trend of lower funding for prison institutions during a period of continued population expansions. This has often led to prison systems jettisoning rehabilitative programs as extravagant expenses and searching for ways to reduce populations they can no longer afford to maintain.

The State of California's medical and mental health care was placed under judicial receivership for being judged woefully inadequate in providing acceptable levels of care when U.S. District Judge Thelton E. Henderson ruled in a class action lawsuit (*Plata v. Schwarzenegger*) that the system was "broken beyond repair." The court found the medical care being provided was a violation of the Eighth Amendment of the U.S. Constitution, which forbids cruel and unusual punishment of the incarcerated. Problems are undoubtedly worsened by a Nation-al health care crisis that leads to the incarceration of individuals that could not afford and/or did not have access to virtually any kind of healthcare entering a system that then is expected to provide for all needed medical/psychiatric care once they are incarcerated. States across the nation have become engaged in efforts to release inmates because they cannot afford to maintain their ever-increasing numbers (Richburg & Surdin, 2008).

The safety of existing institutions has also become increasingly questioned as initial efforts to save money by reducing staffing have led to environments that place staff and the general public at an increased risk. For example, the Federal Bureau of Prisons has long maintained unusually low levels of staffing relative to inmates housed in that system as compared to state systems and touted itself as a model prison system for states to emulate. However, it has been acknowledged that to maintain even its relatively low staffing rate prevalent in the year 2000 at present would require the addition of 9,000 staff. Even the Director of Federal Bureau of Prisons has been forced to publicly acknowledge in 2008 that the inmate to staff ratio has become dangerously imbalanced owing to inadequate funding.

The cyclical nature of the criminal justice system historically suggests that although the offender population may not have entirely peaked at this point, that an increasing emphasis on rehabilitating, rather than merely housing, offenders is likely to follow in the next decade. At present, however, efforts seem to be more focused on quickly easing population pressures by searching for ways to divert placing more people in prison or justifying the increasingly early release of those already incarcerated. Efforts to reduce somewhat the recent push towards more stringent and less flexible sentencing is also beginning to occur as well (White, 2008).

PSYCHOLOGISTS IN CORRECTIONS

With the growth in the correctional population have come increases in the population of psychologists dedicated to this specialty area. This is not surprising given the high rates of mental health problems that exist in the Nation's jail and prison inmates. It is estimated that 44 percent of males and 61 percent of females in Federal prisons have mental health problems, as well as 55 percent of males and 73 percent of females in State Prisons. In local jails 63 percent of males and 75 percent of females are estimated to suffer from some type of mental health issue (Bureau of Justice Statistics, 2006b). The number of full-time psychologists employed in State and Federal correctional settings in the United States increased from 1,144 at the beginning of 1992 (Camp & Camp, 1992) to 1,656 at the beginning of 1995 (Camp & Camp, 1995). This amounts to an astounding 45 percent increase in the space of three years. This trend has continued in recent years and (it should be noted) excludes the much greater number of psychologists employed by counties, cities and/or on a contract basis who have undoubtedly grown proportionately. Increasing understanding of what types of programs may produce effective reductions in recidivism along with realizations that mere incarceration actually increases the chances of future criminologic behavior thrusts psychologists into the role of being able to influence production and refinement of effective treatment programs. The increasing numbers of professionals in the field should lead to greater opportunities for professional discourse and sharing of information so as to further legitimize the work being performed in this field.

It is perhaps unfortunate that there are relatively few widely published research articles available documenting advances in this field given the large number of programs that exist on national, state and local levels. There is also a danger in the continuation of this practice in that some programs of lessened effectiveness (e.g., boot camps), but with greater inherent public appeal, may proliferate while more effective ventures may suffer from their lack of public support in winning additional attention and expansion. Given the level of training in research that psychologists typically encounter during their formal education, we are probably unique in our ability to construct solid programs and provide effective review of same. The only danger to the continued and increasing presence of psychologists in the correctional field is our own complacency in furthering the effectiveness of pro-grams, and the public knowledge of them.

As for the current state of affairs, there appears no doubt that the perspective psychologists offer in correctional systems is both valuable and unique. Generally, the services given, while not always well understood by other staff members, leads to the psychologist being appreciated and at least complicitly recognized. The trend in the future is likely to involve increasing administrative responsibilities and the delegation of clinical duties to lesser trained mental health profes-sionals, but with increasing efforts to organize and cooperate, psy-chologists can easily secure an increasing role in the criminal justice system. Psychologists are also becoming more involved in more administrative tasks that deviate from our traditional role as evidenced by some of our colleagues moving to positions of higher general authority, including that of institutional warden. Indeed, a recent Director of the Federal Bureau Introduction of Prisons, Kathleen Hawk-Sawyer, was herself a clinical psychologist by training.

EFFECTIVENESS OF CORRECTIONAL TREATMENT

Assessing the effectiveness of treatment programs provided to prison inmates is made difficult by the great variability in quality of these efforts. There is often a tendency to give lip service to treatment, which actually involves few elements of standard programs given in other settings, and instead focus primarily on crisis management. Thus, the education and experience of treatment providers, the degree of contact with staff members, the appropriateness of treatment for the individuals involved and other factors not only vary, but can be diffi-cult to discern in published studies. The result, I believe, is that many figures that are currently available are likely to underestimate the true potential of well-coordinated programs.

Andrews et al. (1990) looked at 154 studies of correctional treatment and their effects on inmate recidivism. They found that correctional treatment efforts were most effective when matched according to the risk level and treatment needs of the offender. In fact, the effect of appropriate correctional services (e.g., drug treatment for chemically dependent offender) was three times that of unspecified correctional services, although even this was found to be better than nothing at all.

The providing of services inappropriate for the offender or providing no services at all was found to provide similar, negative results across all studies reviewed.

Andrews, Bonta and Hoge (1990) specifically examined the issue of matching treatment services to the degree of risk represented by individual inmates. High risk inmates are more likely, statistically, to recidivate upon release. Table 1.1 reproduces a summary of their findings. It was found that more intensive degrees of treatment correlated with the risk level of inmates, such that high risk inmates benefitted most from greater intensity treatments while low risk inmates actually showed a greater likelihood of recidivism as the intensity of their treatment exposure increased. The significance of this finding is considerable in that low risk inmates have traditionally been viewed as more open and responsive to treatment interventions, while higher risk inmates are less

TABLE 1.1
THE EFFECT OF OFFENDER RISK LEVEL AND TREATMENT
INTENSITY IN FOUR STUDIES ON TREATMENT OUTCOME
EXPRESSED IN RECIDIVISM PERCENTAGE
(ANDREWS, BONTA & HOGE, 1990).

Study	Risk Level	Level of Treatment	
		Minimal	Intensive
O'Donnell et al. (1971)	Low	16	22
	High	78	56
Baird et al. (1979)	Low	3	10
	Medium	18	13
	High	37	18
Andrews & Kiessling (1980)	Low	12	17
	High	58	31
Andrews & Freisen (1987)	Low	12	29
	High	92	25

likely to be engaged in significant treatment efforts. The findings suggest that we may actually benefit from leaving low risk inmates to themselves while focusing greater attention and funding to targeting what has heretofore been those most likely to be discarded as beyond help.

The other significant conclusion that can be reached from Table 1.1 is that, when appropriately provided, correctional treatment can dramatically reduce recidivism rates of even the most difficult cases.

There are some caveats to this conclusion, however. Treatment has been demonstrated to be ineffective or even counterproductive if it is not matched to the specific needs of the inmate (Andrews et al., 1990). Additionally, there is mounting evidence that involving inmates high in assessed psychopathy (see Chapter 3) in treatment efforts may actually serve to increase their likelihood of committing future crime, especially violent crime (Rice, Harris, & Cormier, 1992; Rice, 1997). It has been noted that psychopaths are more likely to prematurely terminate treatment efforts (Ogloff, Wong, & Greenwood, 1990), but evidence that continued treatment may have reverse effects is more recent. Baumeister, Smart and Boden (1996) hypothesized that treatment may raise the self-esteem of psychopaths and lead to a consequent increase in their tendency to engage in aggression. It has also been suggested that psychopaths may learn empathy and social skills in treatment programs that allow them to more effectively manipulate, deceive and abuse others (Harris, Rice, & Cormier, 1994). The findings clearly complicate the results displayed in Table 1.1. Although those at highest risk of reoffending may offer our most successful route to treatment effectiveness, there is clearly a subset of these individuals for whom treatment cannot be recommended. Identification of which group an offender best represents will likely require special assessment techniques which will need to become more refined in the future. Our success in differentiating these groups, then, would also seem to enable us to improve even further on the already impressive demonstrations of treatment effectiveness shown in Table 1.1.

CONTRIBUTION OF PSYCHOLOGY IN CORRECTIONS

True rehabilitation of prison inmates is always a secondary consideration behind maintaining institutional security and the safety of those within. There has been an increasing political push in recent years to look "tough" on crime, with the only legislative outlet for demonstrating such a commitment being enhancing the length of sentences and demanding that sentences handed out are actually served. While this may be successful in building a reputation for law and order and eliciting the political support of constituents, it also creates a burgeoning population of inmates that are serving increasingly lengthy sentences.

Past research has shown us that lengthening inmates sentences actually increases their chances of recidivating upon release (Andrews et al., 1990). What is needed is an organized and systematic approach that can develop and evaluate systems for reducing recidivism and understanding criminal behavior. The ultimate goal of preventing and reducing societal crime may then become increasingly possible with the knowledge gleaned being applied at the juvenile level to "at risk" populations.

One such area where this has actually occurred has been in the proliferation of "drug courts" wherein first-time drug offenders are offered treatment and supervised probation in lieu of incarceration. Offenders plead guilty, agree to take part in treatment, regular drug screenings and regular reporting to a court judge for at least one year. Should the offender fail to comply with one or more of the requirements they may be removed from the drug court and incarcerated at the judge's discretion. The first drug court was created in Miami-Dade County, Florida, in 1989, as a response to the growing crack cocaine problem effecting the city (Goldkamp & Weiland, 1993). It was designed such that nonviolent offenders could receive treatment versus incarceration. By 1999 there were 472 drug courts in the nation and by 2005 that number had increased to 1262 with another 575 drug courts in the planning stages. Such courts now operate in all 50 states (Rempel et al., 2003). In 2003 the Center for Court Innovation released a report which analyzed the impact of the drug court system in the State of New York (Center for Court Innovation, 2003). Recidivism rates for those participating in the drug court were found to be 29 percent lower over three years when compared to the same types of offenders that did not enter the drug court. The same study estimated a cost savings of $254 million in incarceration costs by diverting 18,000 non-violent drug offenders into state drug courts. The State of California estimates the state saves $90 million per year through their drug courts (Judicial Council of California, 2006). Many other states have experienced similar results (Roman, Townsend & Bhati, 2003).

In reviewing the literature it is clear that many innovative and defensible rehabilitative efforts have been devised over the years under the direction of talented psychologists. It is just as clear, however, that published documentation and evaluation of these efforts has been lacking. It is not enough to effectively manage and treat those specifically assigned to us. We must establish ourselves as behavioral scien-

tists with evolving programs of increasing effectiveness for our ultimate goal of reducing crime to be accomplished. This, in turn, necessitates professional collaboration through the use of ongoing evaluation and publication of our programs.

There are times when we may be reluctant to call attention to efforts that seem to fall short of their desired effectiveness, but when we
become accomplices to the masking of such failures we only prolong
the popularization of ineffective treatments with the eventual disillusionment of the public about our ability to offer anything of value.
There are too many efforts in existence capable of demonstrating positive results and too many directions for future development of effective interventions to anchor oneself to a sinking ship. Greater collaboration amongst professionals in the field can ensure the maximal success and continued growth of psychology's positive influence in this
most challenging field. The contribution of psychology to this field, I
believe, remains in its infancy with endless possibilities for success.

In the pages that follow, an attempt is made to outline some of the
unique characteristics of doing clinical work in the correctional area,
and the various roles psychologists commonly occupy. We then turn
to a discussion of how to establish appropriate and effective working
relationships with inmates, as well as methods of detecting and dealing with manipulativeness and malingering. Issues related to forming
beneficial alliances with other institutional staff are then discussed and,
then, a final discussion of issues one will have to confront in working
in the correctional field. Throughout the text I have attempted to
demonstrate significant points with real-life examples. The present
publication does not seek to encourage or discourage potential new
entrants to the field, but to help those contemplating such a choice to
be able to make a more informed decision. For those al-ready in the
field it is hoped the subsequent pages provide some useful information
and/or spur an interest in solidifying the empirical underpinnings of
the area of correctional psychology.

Chapter 2

ENVIRONMENTAL DIFFERENCES
IN CORRECTIONS

IT IS SOMEWHAT UNNERVING to step into a prison environment for the first time for most people. We realize at some level that
we have entered into another dimension, one that relatively few members of our society ever have direct contact with. We also realize that
in doing so we have not only left behind a more familiar environment,
but also one that we believe to be much safer. As we enter into a prison
our anxiety level rises and we become much more keenly aware of
what is going on around us. This is, of course, an adaptive response to
potential dangers around us. It can, however, make it difficult to concentrate on being empathic and understanding to those in emotional
distress. Fortunately, with time we begin to feel more comfortable in
this new environment as we become more familiar with it. The anxiety, or in macho terms the autonomic stimulation, begins to fade over
time. It never, however, dissipates entirely, nor should it. For if it were
that would be when you would find yourself truly being in a more dangerous situation. Instead, it becomes part of the work environment.
Make no mistake about it, correctional work is a stressful job regardless of your position. The constant stress of maintaining clear awareness of your surroundings at all times can easily take its toll over time.
That is not to say that it is unbearable or unmanageable, but it needs
to be acknowledged and accepted from the outset, so that its deleterious effects can be most effectively kept under control.

As one spends more time in such an environment it begins to feel
more natural and comfortable. You become aware of emergency pro-

cedures that offer a measure of self-protection and also realize that the environment is not as dire as your mind may have first imagined. In fact, one comes to recognize it as a mini society unto itself. Most prison facilities are remarkably self-sufficient and have available within them all the basics of life – dining facilities, sleeping quarters, medical treatment, barber, library, schooling, jobs. In today's most effectively run correctional environments, efforts are put forth to keep in-mates as occupied as possible. By minimizing idle time, the opportunities for inmates to ruminate about their environment and direct their negative energies into efforts to organize themselves towards destructive ends are minimized. The inmates are quite active through much of their day in assigned job activities, just as most of us remain involved in our daily work activities. This significantly cuts down on problems within the inmate population by keeping them too occupied to focus or organize their negative energies towards creating problems.

There is actually quite a degree of variability amongst correctional institutions. Most of them focus on a particular security level of inmate, ranging from minimum to low to medium to high to maximum security. The environment you work in, as well as the problems you will encounter, will vary considerably depending on the security level of your institution. Minimum security institutions are typically quite open and have inmates serving relatively brief sentences for non-violent offenses. These environments are relatively relaxed, with a minimum of tension in evidence among the inmates or the staff members. Rather than dealing with hardcore antisocial personalities here you may find yourself more involved with more chronic neurotic inmates, inmates experiencing acute anxiety disturbance from being housed in a foreign environment and inmates experiencing depression from being forcibly separated from their friends, families and, in some cases, their livelihoods. Additionally, the level of supervision is usually mild enough in such settings that it allows the inmates just enough freedom to allow them to get into greater trouble.

Those with particularly poor impulse control and lack of common sense may find the absence of razor wire fences and armed personnel in a minimum security setting just too tempting. While from a societal perspective an escape from such a facility is minor, when the inmate is later apprehended it will still be taken quite seriously. Typically, it will be sufficient to add several years to their sentences as well as upgrade them to a higher security institution. For example, I once dealt with a relatively young inmate who was getting close to being released. Approximately two months prior to getting out, he could not help himself and decided to leave the facility one evening for a romantic rendezvous with an acquaintance of the opposite sex in a local motel. Unfortunately for him, the staff was tipped off that he was missing (probably by a jealous inmate with either no such opportunity or with relatively more anal retentive traits). The interloper was apprehended and transported to a high security institution for disciplinary action. As a result of this midnight escapade the inmate bought himself approximately nine months in a segregation cell and an additional two years of prison time in a medium security institution.

Such stories are not rare, but may point to a need for a psychologist or other staff member to occasionally loan a piece of their superegos to prevent such shortsighted and foolish behavior. As a psychologist in a minimum security setting you will become aware of inmates who have motivations to commit such acts by receiving word of an inmates family members illness, through staff or other inmates reporting an inmate with severe cabin fever or from the inmate themself who reports that they are struggling to follow the rules, but need a strong authority figure to sway their minds in the proper direction at times. Although one can never know how many escapes are prevented by such interventions, they can save a great deal of problems for the inmate and the staff, as well as keep the cost of confining the inmate down by limiting their length of stay and the degree of supervision required.

Low, medium and high security facilities add increasing degrees of difficulty in escaping, lesser freedom of movement for inmates, greater numbers of barriers to pass through while moving within the compound for both inmates and staff, and increasing past history and future potential for violence amongst the inmates. As one progresses to maximum security inmates there may be no movement allowed outside the individual's cell beyond one hour a day for recreation. Also, as one moves up the security level ladder there is an increasing degree of tension and stress present amongst both the inmates and staff which can lead to the long-term negative effects discussed earlier.

Your client base in corrections also tends to be quite different than other places. You will very often deal with people that do not want anything to do with you. Very often those that may need your help the most will want it the least and those that need it the least will want it the most. It can be a difficult quandary to try to avoid the neurotic that always thinks that they need someone to hold their hand while trying to convince the psychotic that they really may have some problems that you could help them with. If you do not understand and accept how the population differs from the typical outpatient clientele that we are most often trained to treat, it can be a very frustrating state of affairs. Ultimately maintaining a matter of fact, parental type of tough love approach to handling all inmates is most often effective. This means making some function more independently than they think they can, while forcing others to submit to your judgments of their mental health, regardless of their opinion.

INTERPERSONAL ENVIRONMENT

The general interpersonal atmosphere that exists in the correctional environment varies greatly from institution to institution and over periods of time within any given setting. Generally speaking, staff members are pleasant to work with, interested in doing a good job, and competent in their positions. The quality of worker and their willingness to work, I believe, is generally higher in this setting than in most bureaucratic organizations. The reason for this is twofold: (1) Employee applicants are screened more thoroughly due to the sensitive nature of the employment setting; (2) Basic personality patterns which attract someone to the law enforcement field tend to include a respect for authority, and a general belief in fairness. There is also, of course, those that are attracted to the field due to more sadistic personal tendencies which are empowered by the inherent power of being in command over prisoners. Such individuals, if not excluded during the initial screening process, should be discovered and terminated early into their careers if the organization is being properly and professionally run.

Unfortunately, the same cannot always be said for the quality of management in such systems. Typically, higher level supervisors are those that did well in entry-level positions and received promotions. The skill sets needed to make a good supervisor are quite different than those that allow one to be a good officer. Additionally, supervisors in these systems are often much less educated than would be the case in another similar structure in the private sector. The quality of supervisory training is usually poor or largely non-existent. As pointed out in Chapter 1 the prison industry has expanded to an incredible degree in recent years. This has required the building of countless new prisons and, obviously, the need for many new supervisors and leaders. It is an unfortunate consequence of this boom that an increasing percentage of such leaders are incompetent to perform their duties. Compounding this situation is the insular nature of most prison systems in which all promotions are carried out within their own ranks, preventing other perspectives from being brought in and correcting shortcomings or blindspots developed over time from being identified and eliminated. For example, the California Prison System has much experience in dealing with gang issues that have more gradually come to permeate the ranks of other prison systems, which have been far too reluctant in asking for assistance and/or utilizing staff from California already experienced in handling such problems. The Federal Prison System, for example, has been reluctant to admit the loss of its former status as a model penal system and ask for outside assistance in managing a population that has changed radically in recent years (Butterfield, 2004).

Within the correctional field, as in all areas of law enforcement, there is a sense of shared duty. Each individual employee works within their own speciality area, perhaps, but all are trained and willing to respond to whatever extent is necessary to help out a fellow employee who finds themselves in a position of imminent danger. As in any large organization, there are arguments and ongoing feuds between and within departments, but in an emergency situation, ones' thoughts quickly turn to protecting staff, all staff, from potential harm from inmates. After all, if you should find yourself in a life-threatening situation with an inmate you probably would not be concerned about which staff member came to your aid, as long as someone did. Likewise, training and commitment to duty inevitably drown out any petty animosities that may exist when a crisis situation arises. Your willingness to accept this code of conduct and to actively practice it will also win you respect from the staff of other departments. As will be discussed in a later chapter, many staff have a vague distrust of the psychologist. Some feel we are there to help the inmates and are really on their side, therefore, we are not to be trusted any more than the inmates themselves. The psychologist, then, often has a greater burden of proving themselves committed to the overarching goals of the institution than do staff members in other specialty areas.

I can recall in my own experience a particular department head who transferred into the institution where I worked a couple of months after I was initially hired. The staff member in question did not seem to trust me, and he seemed to want nothing to do with me. Although our various duties occasionally found us close by each other we learned to largely ignore each other as if the other did not exist. One morning as I was walking across the compound I saw staff members running in my direction. In the front was this particular staff member who yelled up ahead that another staff member in a nearby department had triggered an alarm for emergency assistance. Having received the information, I spun around and took the lead, charging into the department where the alarm had been initiated. I was the first one on the scene. As is often the case, the alarm turned out to be a false one. However, my being the first to arrive on the scene was not lost on the department head who had heretofore chose to overlook my existence. In the coming days and weeks, I suddenly became acknowledged and accepted by this staff member. Such is the case when you work in the correctional field. You will have to prove yourself as truly trustworthy and committed through your actions, words and behaviors.

Oftentimes the psychologist will have to win over other staff members one by one. In many cases, you may not know what won them over, but be assured, as a psychologist in a correctional institution you occupy a high profile position. Staff members will watch you and will notice the things that you do. After all, unlike most of the other senior level staff who rose from the front lines through hard work and determination, psychologists are often seen as having been granted their positions by virtue of privileged backgrounds. Though this is usually untrue, I have decided that proving oneself in this arena is the best tactic to take. After all, if one merely does their job appropriately, this will be relatively easily accomplished.

THE INSTITUTIONAL WORK ENVIRONMENT

The impression most people have of a prison are of large rows of cells with inmates banging against the bars and yelling loudly in between aggressive assaults on staff members. In short, an environment of chaos and desperation. This is an unfortunate consequence of media coverage that focuses almost entirely on the worst prisons in existence at the worst times. The presence of news media at most institutions is ordinarily confined to instances of riots or major assaults, coverage of staff corruption cases or, rarely, coverage of the confinement of high profile cases upon entering prison. Additionally, many scenes of prison conditions depicted on television or described in the print media are based more on descriptions of prisons in developing nations than those in the United States because those prisons are more accessible to the news media and because their conditions are more "newsworthy." Even scenes of Turkish prisons or Russian prison camps, however, become associated in the public's eyes with prison conditions elsewhere. This is much akin to following an individual around for days at a time with a video camera waiting for them to show glimpses of their human shortcomings that can then be displayed in an "expose" on their poor character in a five-minute news segment. The only other glimpses the general public obtains of prison conditions are in theatrical movies which similarly contort reality to enhance the dramatic impact of their presentations.

Actual conditions in most prison institutions are surprisingly mundane. There is an undeniable variability in prison conditions across facilities in the United States, but the worst prisons may not even be as bad as most people's conception of the typical prison environment. The environment of prison institutions is, for most people, surprisingly quiet, organized and calm. There are strict rules of behavior that prevent inmates from engaging in significantly disruptive or even potentially disruptive actions. Although riots and major group disturbances can occur on rare occasions, most of the time inmate actions are controlled to such a large extent that the organization of these behaviors is made difficult. Their abilities to congregate into unauthorized and unsupervised groups is prevented, for example, and any inflammatory remarks they make that could inflame the emotions of the general population are simply not tolerated. Such conduct will usually result in their being separated and isolated from other inmates. In fact, most inmates are far from interested in participating in these kinds of destructive activities. Instead, many of them are as interested as the staff in maintaining as orderly an environment as possible. After all, in the event of disruption, they are at greater risk than the staff. If they participate in the disturbance, they could be placing themselves in physical danger from staff efforts to regain control of the situation or even from their fellow inmates' unleashed aggressions. In addition, their involvement will likely result in their receiving additional prison time and/or placement in a higher security environment with greater personal restrictions. Obviously, the shorter the inmates sentence and the lower security environment they are in, the less inclined they are to want to participate in any disruptive activities. As a result, these types of disruptions are almost entirely confined to medium and high security institutions, each of which has greater levels of restrictiveness and procedures to prevent and/or minimize inmates disruptive potential. It also should be emphasized that even when a disruption occurs, the problems are often precipitated and prolonged by a relatively small number of inmates. In fact, many inmates resort to retreating to their cells quite voluntarily for their own protection until the problem is resolved.

Since most inmates are disinterested in creating such problems or even participating in them is not surprising, if one keeps in mind the basic self-centeredness most inmates possess. Cooperative group behavior, even for purposes of destruction and defiance, is not in keeping with their natural tendencies towards isolation and independence. The two most likely exceptions to this are probably the hard-core antisocial and the gang-affiliated offender. In the first instance, you will likely be dealing with a penitentiary inmate (high to maximum security) with a long sentence and an opinion that they have nothing to lose. Any opportunity to strike at established authority may be welcomed. After the initial excitement dies down, these inmates represent the most significant threat both to other inmates and to any staff that may have been taken hostage.

The gang affiliated offender is one who has probably been involved since early adolescence in delinquent activities which almost always involved some level of cooperative effort in a bid to establish some sense of achievement and identity in their social group. They usually are incapable of initiating large group disturbances unless there are sufficient numbers of fellow gang members present and, even then, will typically be too busy directing their energies towards rival gang members and too unable to cooperate with them to focus themselves on violence directed towards the institution itself. Additionally, measures are usually taken to control and separate members of the same gang, whenever possible, with potential leaders of violent actions being particularly segregated from their fellow group members. For an excellent overview and discussion of the factors that lead to inmate riots and disturbances, as well as steps to take in preventing and managing them, see Sherman (1996).

THE DEPARTMENTAL WORK ENVIRONMENT

Psychology departments are generally autonomous organizations within the overall prison institution. As the work that occurs there is in such contrast to much of the rest of the immediate organization that is necessarily focused on control and management of inmates, there is much independence afforded. While there are specific duties the psychology staff are responsible for, there are ample opportunities for one to utilize and develop one's own personal style in carrying out these activities. In contrast to media depictions and discussions of inmate uprisings, the day-to-day atmosphere within the psychology department is really rather pleasant and relaxed. There is a calmness that tends to result within the institution because of the behavioral limits on the inmates freedom which forces them to control their emotions and behaviors to a greater extent than they have ever been required. In fact, it is a joke within this author's family that when I arrive home from work to the natural chaos and noise that result from having children that I sometimes express a desire to be back at the calm, quiet environment of the prison in which I work. That is not to suggest that this is always the case, however, and the environment can be starkly different in institutions that are inadequately staffed and/or organized.

The quality of interactions with inmates can be surprisingly positive and of good substance. There is obviously great variability across and within institutions, but the majority of inmates are quite receptive to the institution psychologist. The primary exceptions to this would be institutions at the highest security level where inmates are more likely to be hostile towards you just as they are to all authority figures and institutions in which there is a large and strong gang presence that will often tend to sanction those members who interact too positively with authority figures. There are places, however, where influential members of typically disruptive gangs become involved in treatment and lead to a partial acceptance of the psychologist into their social milieu, erasing the stigma of treatment involvement.

Some inmates are attracted to the psychologist for intellectual conversation, some are drawn to speak with you because they do not feel they can trust anyone else to unload their concerns or thoughts on, some come looking for advice, some come with hidden agendas of trying to obtain medications, have contact with a member of the opposite sex, to get certification that they are too "crazy" to be given a cellmate or for some other hidden agenda. Some inmates appear to want contact with a parental-type figure they can use as a role model, or perhaps as a replacement for the positive parental model they lacked in their childhoods. These groups, including those with demonstrated mental health problems, construct the vast majority of your client base.

It has been my finding that inmates tend to be quite appreciative of groups offered through the psychology program. I have personally conducted groups on anger management, for example, in a wide variety of inpatient and outpatient settings in my career. I must admit I was initially apprehensive as to what inmates might be attracted to such a group offering. In the end, however, I have found inmate groups on this topic include participants who are more involved and ask more thought-provoking questions than any other population with which I have worked. The level of cognitive comprehension is often fairly concrete, but I have found inmates able to analyze more deeply their motivations with the proper instruction, and to respond well to cognitive behavioral-type intervention strategies. Such groups predominantly consist of voluntary participants and they have more time to reflect on the group content in the hours and days following a group meeting, which leads to the possibility of significant cognitive and behavioral effects of the groups.

CONFIDENTIALITY ISSUES

Inmates often make the assumption that anything they say to the psychologist is completely confidential. As such, they can reveal information they would not dare share with anyone else on the correctional staff. While there may be some level of confidentiality present, the exceptions are far greater in a correctional environment. In all cases, anything the inmate shares which may impact on the security of the institution is considered public information and should never be maintained in confidence. Although this may seem like a relatively limited exception, it is open to great individual interpretation. For example, while discussing with "Inmate Jones" regarding his adjustment into the prison environment, he may slip and mention that his cellmate is manufacturing intoxicants in their cell. Inmate Jones insists that he is not involved and does not use the homemade alcoholic beverages and invokes your advice on how to end the situation. Should you violate confidentiality and inform the correctional staff? If you inform the correctional staff, Inmate Jones will likely be charged with possessing the intoxicants along with his cellmate since it is located in their shared cell. He may be given disciplinary segregation ("the hole"), and receive disciplinary action for something he not could control, and was actually seeking help with. Alternately, the Correctional Staff may acknowledge his coming forward and punish only his cellmate. In this instance, though, you risk that Inmate Jones was setting up his roommate because he did not like him and/or Inmate Jones being labeled a "snitch" by other inmates who may then target him for harassment or physical assault. If you keep the information confidential, someone could get physically harmed by consuming the beverages, an inmate might become unruly "under the influence" and hurt himself or others or even incite a riot. Most importantly, the inmate has placed a wedge between you and the other correctional staff. You will have sided with the inmate and opened yourself up to being blackmailed about it into more gradual, but consistent movements into questionable, if not outright illegal, behaviors.

Some might suggest that you make the manner of resolving the situation the inmates choice – "either you tell the correctional staff, Mr. Jones, or I will have to." In this case, if the inmate takes the lesser of two evils and informs the correctional staff himself, he will be labeled a "snitch" by other inmates. This label will open him up to retribution from not only his cellmate, but his cellmate's comrades and numerous other inmates that resent anyone with such a label. Ultimately, the inmate may be physically assaulted or, in some environments, killed for his cooperation. If he is more fortunate and he is in a system with numerous resources he may be transferred elsewhere for his own protection. However, this often means moving away from family and friends in the local community, making the maintenance of such ties all the more difficult. Additionally, the inmate will always wonder when the label will find him in the new environment through the inmate grapevine. The example demonstrates how a behavior of no consequence in the outside environment and a fairly minor infraction even on the inside environment can cause great angst to the therapist. The opposite problem also exists wherein you are considered by an inmate to be a member of the law enforcement community and no degree of knowledge or willingness to help is going to convince the inmate to tell you anything about them that you don't already know. As the example above shows, some degree of paranoia towards you is probably healthy from the inmate's perspective. Many inmates already have significant interpersonal trust problems and an impaired ability to establish and/or maintain intimate relationships. Given all this, it is a wonder that inmates speak to correctional psychologists at all!

The problems of determining what is confidential and what is not can present themselves in much more mundane activities that are common in their occurrence. Consider the inmate who enters the institution in a mildly depressed state. According to the policy active in the Federal system, all inmates are screened on admission with a report sent to an administrative "team" involved in coordinating that inmates care. In sending the report you are to note any concerns related to mental health which you may want to do in any event if the inmate's adjustment seems questionable. In effect, their interaction with you from the start possesses no confidentiality.

It has been my experience that as one moves towards the upper end of the security spectrum (minimum to maximum) that you become more likely to see an inmate unwilling to speak with you and you are less likely to see an inmate who is overly trusting. It also is usually the case that the topic of conversation in individual sessions is in regards to relationships, difficulties and situations occurring outside the prison environment. Most inmates are able to blend into the prison environment fairly readily and become routinized to its ways. It is rare than an inmate will discuss institutionally-based difficulties, other than offering complaints about having to remain there or about the unfairness of the rules or staff. In cases where inmates talk about problems with other inmates, it is usually a crisis-oriented situation where they are under significant threat and action on your part will probably need to be taken anyway or an effort to manipulate you into targeting another inmate that they have a personal dispute with for disciplinary action.

In working with inmates, different clinicians utilize varying strategies for dealing with the issue of confidentiality. Some prefer to address the issue candidly with an initial discussion of the nature of confidentiality and its specific exceptions. Others may post a written explanation in the department work area for inmates to see and review. Personally, I prefer not to draw attention to the issue. In the vast majority of cases, promises of confidentiality or no, inmates are going to limit what they are willing to reveal to you. When an inmate engages in greater degrees of self-disclosure it is usually because they are in crisis and they have little concern for the rules of confidentiality. Additionally, if one truly investigates and reflects on the topic you will likely conclude that true confidentiality is an illusion. There are so many situations in which one is required or advised to inform others of the inmate's verbal report that it is difficult to construct an argument that any sanctity of communication exists at all.

Instead of discussing confidentiality issues candidly, then, it is has been my preference to bring them up during those rare sessions in which it appears the inmate is getting ready to reveal information that will almost certainly require disclosure to others on my part. At these times it is wise to advise the inmate that if they reveal information about a particular topic that one suspects they are moving towards that the psychologist would have a professional obligation to notify others. It has been my experience that this approach is appreciated and respected. Additionally, I cannot recall a situation in which this approach seemed to substantially alter what the inmate subsequently revealed. As discussed on the chapter on inmate relations, inmates share extensive information with each other which no doubt sometimes includes what they should and should not tell the psychologist. In my experience, inmates are usually quite aware of the situation and are likely to feel the psychologist is trying to deceive them if issues of confidentiality are brought up prematurely.

THE POWER OF SECRETS AND COMMUNICATION IN A CORRECTIONAL ENVIRONMENT

Maintaining secrets is not a behavior that is foreign to psychologists in any setting. In fact, confidentiality is a prime aspect of our trade that is highly valued by those we serve. Confidentiality of inmate communications can sometimes pose ethical or legal complications, as out-lined above, that can necessitate limited divulging of information to outside parties. As a general rule, though, much of what is discussed is maintained in confidence. Many conversations with other staff will revolve around inmates and many of the inmates they discuss will be those that have had contacts with psychology. Staff members will even approach you with questions on your assessment of certain inmates and advice on how to best interact with them. These are legitimate questions, but it can be difficult to answer without an explanation of some aspects of the inmates cases. As a result, where to draw the line on confidentiality can be hard to decide. You don't want to unneces-sarily reveal information about the inmate, but you also want to main-tain good relations with the staff member and assist in institutional management by responding to their questions.

The environment of a prison is one that can make keeping secrets a more difficult and confusing process than in other work environments. First of all, you are functioning in the realm of law enforcement which is a secretive world unto its own. In a prison, you are most definitely not the only one with secrets to keep. In fact, it appears that everyone, staff and inmate, possess secrets in what amounts to almost a contest to see who can know what and when.

With the added responsibility of EAP provider, you will likely know personal secrets about staff members within the institution. Although confidentiality considerations are more easily decided, it still can make interacting with other staff members or inmates who may wish to dis-cuss that staff member difficult to manage.

Higher level staff members may tell you things about lower level staff members. Lower level staff members may tell you things about higher level staff members. EAP participants may tell you things no one else should know. Inmates may tell you things that are not signif-icant enough to reveal, but impinge on other inmates or institutional operations. Medical services may tell you information that is not to be released to other departments (e.g., HIV cases). Unit staff may tell you information about inmates that can be told to staff, but not the inmates themselves. These are but a few examples of the conundrum a cor-rectional psychologist may face. Sorting it out can be confusing at times.

When you interact with other staff members, it is not uncommon to find out information that some staff know and others do not. Often staff will assume that you know information no one has told you. As a result, it is quite important to be aware of institutional happenings and interact with a large variety of staff to keep abreast of institutional events. Otherwise, you may find yourself faced with a distressed inmate discussing a number of commonly known situations you are unaware of or have an EAP contact with a staff member that talks about many issues of which you are entirely unaware of. If you have other psychologists or staff in your department, it is crucial to keep lines of communication open with all and to encourage everyone to share information they have on a regular basis in both formal and informal discussions.

In larger departments with staff members that operate in numerous different social circles within the institution there can be a rich collection of knowledge to be mined if there exists a sense of basic trust and shared purpose within the department. By the same token, it does not take long for a psychologist in an administrative position over other staff members to completely lose touch with happenings within the institution if they do not spend adequate personal resources communicating with their staff. This will inevitably lead to a failure to anticipate untoward events within the institution that impact the Psychology Department and expose it to be much less effective in assisting with inmate management than it could otherwise be. I believe one must be careful, however, to avoid engaging in what amounts to routine gossiping for to do so compromises your professionalism and others' ability and willingness to trust you. I am always willing to listen to what others have to say, but remain judicious in passing on information myself that is not necessary to do so. A psychologist who cannot resist the temptation to gossip has issues of their own they need to address.

Inmates are ever-present within institutions. Wherever they are they gather information about topics discussed by staff, as well as their general comings and goings. This information is routinely spread and pooled in the inmate population as a whole. If one works within a prison system long enough, you are likely to encounter a situation at some point in which an inmate will share some aspect of knowledge about your activities, habits or personal life that will surprise you. After all, information gathering is constantly being done by both sides. It is my belief that the degree of organization and dissemination of this information may actually be the deciding factor in who truly controls an institution: the inmates or the staff.

One of the roles of staff is to maintain security within the institution which means that they are concerned with anything going on that is not in compliance with official regulations. Given that the prison population consists of many individuals that have made a life's work out of defying authority, there are always sufficient attempts at wrongdoing to keep staff members occupied.

It is important that one does not get too caught up in the individual acts of inmates to notice an organization or pattern to them. Even when inmates do not blatantly impart information verbally to staff, they often will reveal themselves through their behavior. For example, if a sudden run of dangerous weapons are found within the institution that significantly exceeds typical behavior, it is probably a sign that trouble is brewing. The number of weapons found generally reveals how safe the inmates feel within the institution and ought to be one measure of the staff's success in building a relationship with inmates where they at least feel relatively safe from physical attack. One well-observed phenomena that has repeatedly occurred before inmate disturbances has been a significant increase in the amount of commissary items the inmates buy in those institutions that operate commissaries. In fact, tracking of sales is often monitored in many institutions to the point that statistical deviations from the norm attract immediate attention and investigation. Finally, offhanded remarks of inmates may sometimes necessitate being taken more seriously than they may seem to warrant at first glance. One staff member discussed with me how an inmate who worked in her area had subtly suggested that she not come to work the next day. That evening a riot erupted.

Psychologists have no superhuman abilities above and beyond other staff to detect when things are amiss. However, we have extensive specialized training in seeing relationships between different variables, interpreting human behaviors and analyzing complex data sets. Additionally, we have the advantages of often being one step removed from the frontlines of inmate misbehavior and to have experience in distancing ourselves from a situation in order to analyze it from a more rational perspective. This collection of skills and training does make us potentially valuable to institutional administrators in defining problem areas, identifying dangerous situations, and rectifying issues before they grow to increasingly dangerous levels. Finally, you will find while working in this setting that quite often you will find a rash of complications developing amongst your chronic mentally ill inmate when tensions arise to the near-breaking point. They will often find reasons to request isolation to relieve real or contrived symptoms brought about by fears for their safety as the environment around them becomes increasingly unstable. When several normally stable inmates begin reporting in problems, the astute practitioner should begin asking questions. If an appropriate relationship has been established, these inmates will usually be willing to provide crucial information that can allow problems to be diverted.

The fuel we need to accomplish the task of assisting with institutional management on both the individual and organizational level is information. I believe the informed and judicious prison administrator will allow the institutional psychologist access to a wide range of information about the institution above and beyond that which is clearly within the domain of psychology practice and use the psychologist as a resource. Of course, this assumes that the institutional psychologist is competent and experienced in their duties. If they are, they can prove to be an invaluable resource. If they are not, they can be more trouble than they are worth.

Regardless of one's technical expertise in corrections or the field of law, however, the psychologist who is a good communicator, listener and networker within any institution will find their basic duties easier to accomplish and will prove to be a potent resource for the astute administrator to utilize. By the same token, the effective psychologist makes known to their superiors when they have concerns or significant observations about the institution to share, rather than waiting to be asked. This ensures useful information finds it way to those in charge whether they choose to use it or not. When the information proves to be valuable, it helps to build the psychologists credibility. When the information is unreliable or invalid, the feedback the psychologist receives is often useful in developing their understanding of inmates and correctional facilities. In either case it ends up being a winning endeavor. In my experience, those psychologists who are most likely to find themselves dissatisfied with this career field or unfulfilled in distinguishing themselves as knowledgeable and valuable are those who are too insecure to admit that they do not know everything about working in this type of environment and, therefore, never learn the skills and information that could help them to excel. Working within a correctional institution brings with it a blend of legal, criminal justice, health and other disciplines that each have a rich and diverse structure and history. This, too, is information that can aid an effective psychologist who enters the field with an openness to new knowledge and experience.

Chapter 3

ROLES OF THE CORRECTIONAL PSYCHOLOGIST

WITHIN THE CORRECTIONAL ENVIRONMENT there are numerous responsibilities that the correctional psychologist has, only some of which may be related to the traditional role of providing individual and group therapy. The overall responsibility of the psychologist is to provide for the mental health needs of the institution, of course. How this is defined and carried out, however, can vary tremendously from one correctional system/institution to another and even from one psychologist to another. Some of the roles that must be fulfilled in virtually any institution are the diagnosis and management of mentally ill inmates, psychological assessments/evaluations for courts and other legal bodies, assessments of violence and suicidal potential, crisis intervention, personnel evaluation and crisis intervention, and lastly, if time permits, individual and group therapy. Of course, since one is operating within a public institution, administrative and paperwork requirements are often a central duty as well.

MANAGEMENT CONSULTANT

In a more global manner, psychologists can serve as a monitor of the institutional environment and attempt to ensure that humane and appropriate handling of inmates occurs routinely, pointing out to staff members and administrators possible exceptions that should be addressed to prevent further problems from developing. I am not suggesting that we are the most moral or decent of the staff working within the correctional environment that needs to monitor the behavior of others, but we do tend to approach inmates from a very different perspective from much of the staff in other departments whose background is more likely to be in law enforcement and criminal justice. These other fields, though worthy, do not always have strong em-phases on good psychological practices for dealing with inmates be-cause they focus more on short-term issues of who gets locked up and how, rather than on how to manage such individuals over a long period of time and in large groups. The psychologists knowledge of the mental functioning of impaired individuals is particularly relevant. Sometimes those with mental illness may need to be treated for minor misbehaviors in ways that differ from full-functioning inmates. Clearly, the psychologist would have the predominant input in such cases.

SUICIDE PREVENTION

It may commonly be believed that suicide is an ever-present phenomena in our Nation's jails, and this is obviously going to be a concern to any psychologist working in the corrections arena. It is not hard to surmise why a 19-year-old inmate given a life sentence after a history of aggression and alienation during adolescence might lack a strong will to live and contemplate the act of suicide. Many crisis contacts that occur within an institution will involve inmates with some level of depression and hopelessness over their situation. In most instances, the institutional psychologist may be the only person that the inmate is able to talk to about feelings, frustrations and thoughts, and in whose absence such thoughts might well culminate into a suicidal attempt.

Oftentimes an opportunity to discuss the situation with an empathic listener can serve to defuse the inner turmoil of the inmate to safer levels that permit a gradual adjustment to their situation. In some cases, repeated contacts which are gradually terminated and/or psychoactive medications may be necessary. Instances of depression are most common when the inmate first arrives in the institution either right after their arrest or just after sentencing. It is important to take care to recognize the level of depression that may be present in the newly incarcerated and for those identified as having problems, an opportunity for follow-up should be given. Obviously, acutely suicidal individuals will require immediate intervention and ongoing observation. For any inmate about whom I have concerns with regards to their level of depression, I routinely schedule a follow-up within a time frame specified by the degree of concern I had in the course of the initial assessment to further assess whether they are adjusting to their situation or will need assistance to do so. In the vast majority of cases, adjustment is proceeding normally. However, it should be noted that most inmates have trouble trusting the psychologist upon their initial entrance into the institution.

If you have some concerns about an inmate and merely give them the opportunity to contact you at a later time if they so desire, they probably will not do so even when they should. On the other hand, I have found that an expression of concern and a promise to follow up in two weeks if I have not heard from them first builds a great deal of trust that the concern in them is genuine. Even if they do not require services at follow-up, a positive relationship with that inmate is established which may become an important asset later in that they will feel comfortable approaching the psychologist for assistance if it becomes necessary and will also likely express their positive feelings towards the department to other needy inmates. As stressed in other areas of this book, inmates talk amongst themselves about all staff and all departments. If your "word of mouth" is good, it will make your job easier, particularly when responding to difficult inmates in crisis situations. You will be amazed that even highly aggressive inmates will often freely cooperate with you and calm down if they have come to see you as someone who is trustworthy and genuine.

An important part of one's responsibilities in the prevention of inmate suicides, then, is a thorough and regular screening of all new incarcerates. In addition, effective prevention will likely involve the training of other staff members in recognizing the signs of depression and suicidal risk. After all, in a large institution with relatively few psychologists you are unlikely to personally recognize the potential risk in an inmate unless he is referred by a staff member with more frequent contact with him or if the inmate approaches you himself. A demonstration of the effectiveness of staff training on awareness of suicidal risk factors is in the United States Federal Bureau of Prisons. The average suicide rate in that system was observed to drop by 50 percent in the five-year period following the introduction of a formal program for training all staff members about suicide prevention. The rate dropped an additional 50 percent in the subsequent five-year period after that. This dramatic decline has at least partially been attributed to the correctional staff's learning to recognize and refer inmates in danger of committing suicide before they make such attempts.

The prevention of suicide is an important role that is spearheaded by the correctional psychologist both for humanitarian reasons and also out of legal necessity (O'Leary, 1989; Correia, 2000). In the event of a successful suicide, the possibility of family members filing wrongful death suits is not only possible, but likely. If an institution and/or its psychologist cannot document that some measures have been taken to identify and intervene with inmates at risk of suicide, the financial cost can be considerable. Thus, psychologists may actually provide fiscal, as well as moral, benefits to the institution they serve.

PREVALENCE AND NATURE OF SUICIDE ATTEMPTS

The actual incidence of inmate suicide is considerably lower than one might at first imagine. Lester (1987) reported that the suicide rate amongst all prisoners in the United States was 23.5/100,000 from 19801983. During this same period the rate for males only was 28.7, for Federal inmates 39/100,000 and for states inmates 28/100,000. This was noted to correspond to previous rating periods, therefore, to be rather stable. Rates of suicide have been shown to increase as the length of inmate sentences increase, with death row inmates displaying a rate of approximately 146.5/100,000 (Lester, 1987b). Since these data were published, there has been an increasing realization of the liability institutions have to prevent suicide, accompanied by more organized efforts to preclude them. In fact, in many cases the rate of suicide today may actually be lower among incarcerates than amongst the general non-incarcerated population. The annual rate of suicide reported by the Federal Bureau of Prisons in 1995 (12/100,00) and 1996 (11/100,000) was comparable to the nationally recognized suicide rate (Stafford & Weisheit, 1988; Holinger, 1987) for both men and women (12/100,000), and significantly lower than the national suicide rate for men alone (18/100,000). Similarly, the rate of suicide of all men incarcerated in Federal and State prisons in 1995 was 14.65 (Bureau of Justice Statistics, 1996). By 2002, the rate had dropped further to 14/100,000 (Bureau of Justice Statistics, 2005). Almost half of the jail suicides during the three-year period 2000-2002 occurred during the inmate's first week in custody. Suicides in prisons were much less concentrated in the period close to admission, with only 7 percent of the suicides occurring during the first month.

One reason suicide rates are not higher is the highly structured nature of the institutional environment, which may actually serve to lower stress levels in many individuals as compared to the outside environment. This particularly may be true of those with a genuine mental illness, who may actually experience more comfort and acceptance in prison than they do on the streets. Also, the high prevalence of inmates with antisocial personality disorder and/or narcissistic personality disorder is no secret. These types of criminals do not tend to turn their destructiveness inward, but to blame and attack others when problems ensue in the vast majority of cases.

Although antisocials do not tend to commit suicide, they are often referred to psychologists for threatening to do so or for making actual suicidal gestures. This is part of the manipulativeness of the antisocial and they rarely actually carry through on their threats, regardless of how serious they are taken. It is usually sufficient to find out what the antisocial is trying to get from their suicidal threats and either have it given to them or else make it clear to them that not only will their current tactic not work, but it will additionally have numerous negative consequences. Typically they will calm down and proceed to connive about an alternative method for achieving their objectives.

The inmate with borderline personality disorder is not so easily dismissed. This inmate will command attention for their actions and if they are not taken seriously they will follow their threats with action. The danger, of course, is if they were not genuinely suicidal initially, they are willing to inflict self-harm just to prove your assessment wrong and increase the stakes in their case. The suicidal gestures themselves may also move to progressively more intense and lethal measures if they do not feel that appropriate action has been taken. Oftentimes this will be the inmate that will require some measure of disciplinary action initiated by the psychologist to resolve the situation (at least temporarily). It is important to stress to staff members that if one gives in to these types of manipulation that it can have a very powerful positive reinforcing effect on not only this inmate, but on many others who are intently watching to see if such methods are effective, so that they, too, may use them in the future. Borderline inmates, and

some other manipulative inmates, will often resort to cutting themselves to gain the attention they seek. In the years 1995–1996, the most
popular method of attempted suicide in the United States Federal
System was cutting with 44 percent of those attempting suicide cutting
themselves. Cutting, while dramatic by the introduction of blood it
produces, is also more easily controlled in regards to lethality of the
attempt. This is confirmed by the fact that none of the successful suicides in the Federal System occurring in the same period were by cutting. In fact, 90 percent were by hanging.

It is probably not wise to challenge a cutter's desire to actually commit suicide successfully, but empathic support is often unwanted
and/or ineffective. Instead, a harder line of prevention by the use of
isolation, constant observation, or use of restraints until the "crisis"
passes may be necessary. In most institutions, a procedure is available
for placing an inmate on "suicide watch," in which they are maintained under constant visual supervision. When an inmate cannot be
soothed through psychotherapeutic attempts, is not appropriately referred for disciplinary measures or otherwise persists in being a significant threat to themselves, a period of time in supervised isolation can
be effective in allowing them an opportunity to calm down and give
the psychologist a chance to observe their ongoing behavior so that a
more careful assessment can be made of their rationality and danger-
ousness.

Although often overlooked, the individual put in charge of observing the inmate can be a significant decision as well. There are numerous situations in which the sheer boredom of watching an inmate in a
separate area of the institution will result in the development of an
ongoing dialogue between the inmate and the officer observing. The
officer in this position can thus become a significant asset or liability
in the effective management of the inmate involved. Training of how
to conduct a suicide watch is probably not as important as the psychologist's judgment of the character of the officer selected to perform
the watch. If the psychologist has any question about the individual
selected, it is the psychologists responsibility to see that their concerns
are addressed immediately.

In most cases, a period of 24–36 hours on suicide watch will either
assist in calming the inmate to the point where they can actively engage in psychotherapeutic dialogue, will reveal them to be clearly manipulating, or will show the seriousness of their mental illness and the

need for more intensive treatment either within the institution or through transfer to a psychiatric facility. The range of options available to a practitioner in such a case whereby the inmate is often demanding what they want "or else" is discussed in Correia (2000).

A somewhat unusual trend in corrections has been to have inmates placed on suicide watch kept under the constant visual observation of other inmates (Junker, Beeler & Bates, 2005). These inmate "companions" or "buddies" are selected and superficially trained to observe and summon assistance if the inmate on watch makes attempts to harm themselves. The wide use and general effectiveness of such buddies is likely the result of inmates inappropriately being placed on suicide watch to begin with. Many psychologists, out of inexperience or lack of confidence, will place inmates on watch that are not truly suicidal in an effort to minimize their potential liability if they turn out to be wrong. The idea of a truly suicidal inmate being placed under the supervision of another inmate (done for no other reason than to save the expense of paying a staff member) is a frightening development and would be hard to defend in court if the inmate on watch successfully harmed themselves in some manner. Of particular concern are places housing high security inmates that utilize this practice. ow can one say that a man considered so dangerous to society that they must be incarcerated in a high security prison is nevertheless trustworthy enough to be trusted with another inmate's life?

SEXUAL ASSAULT PREVENTION

The United States Supreme Court, through various decisions, has indicated that prison staff members can be held liable if they know or believe that a harmful act is likely to occur to a specific inmate and take no action to prevent it (deliberate indifference). This concept has been expanded to include a responsibility for the prevention of sexual assault, where possible. The institution psychologist is likely to find the prevention of sexual assault and therapeutic intervention following a sexual assault as one of their assigned duties. In actual practice this role does not occupy a significant portion of time because inmates will typically work out such issues between themselves without alerting staff members and it may be hard to predict in many cases who will be targeted for such abuse. Additionally, where sexual behavior is suspected to exist between inmates it is usually difficult to discern whether any coercive element exists in the absence of an appeal for assistance on the part of at least one of the inmates involved. As is the case with any violent type of behavior, the incidence of such assaults should be expected to increase as one moves to increasingly higher levels of security, such that a psychologist working in a penitentiary will be more likely to be involved in cases than a psychologist in a minimum security setting.

In spite of media portrayals and morbid jokes that imply that sexual assaults are common to the prison environment, best estimates suggest this is not the case in most institutions. It is also likely that only a small percentage of such incidents get reported, however, making confident assessments regarding prevalence difficult. Data from Federal Prison studies indicate that 63 percent of cases of sexual assault are never discovered by staff (Nacci & Kane, 1983). Inmate surveys have found that 29 percent of Federal inmates report having been propositioned while in prison and 30 percent of penitentiary inmates admit to a homosexual experience while incarcerated, though this does not equate with actual sexual assault.

A study of prisons in four Midwestern states found that approximately one in five male inmates reported a pressured or forced sexual incident while incarcerated. About one in ten male inmates reported that they had been raped (Struckman-Johnson & Struckman-Johnson, 2000). Rates for women, who are most likely to be abused by male staff members, vary greatly among institutions. In one facility, 27 percent of women reported a pressured or forced sex incident, while in another facility, 7 percent of women reported instances of sexual abuse.

Rates of HIV are five to ten times as high inside a prison as outside (Dumond & Dumond, 2002), making forced sex a deadly proposition in an environment that provides no methods of preventing the transmission of sexually transmitted diseases. Prisoner rape victims are typically among the most vulnerable members of the population in custody. Male victims are often young, non-violent, first-time offenders who are small, weak, shy, gay or effeminate, and inexperienced in the ways of prison life. Studies suggest that a typical male prison rapist chooses a victim on the basis of a perceived inability of the victim to defend himself (Man & Cronan, 2002). Believing they have no choice, some male prisoners consent to sexual acts to avoid violence. Once attacked, such victims are often marked as targets for further attacks, eventually forcing victims to accept long-term sexual enslavement in order to survive which may include prostitution arrangements with other male prisoners.

The institution psychologist will likely be involved in educating staff members about potential risk factors which make inmates more susceptible to being targeted as victims, and emphasizing the serious nature of such acts. There is sometimes a tendency to believe that inmates get what they deserve and that if they are assaulted in prison, it is their own fault for getting locked up in the first place, or that they must have somehow "asked for it." The myths and misperceptions regarding prison sexual assault thus mimic those that often occur in heterosexual rape in the general community, where victims traditionally have often been given less empathy than they perhaps deserve. In addition to violating the need to provide a safe and humane environment generally for inmates, there is evidence to suggest that sexual assaults and sexual pressure can lead to increasingly serious episodes of violence within the prison itself. The seriousness of assault cases is not only in its direct psychological impact on the victim, then, but also in its potential to contribute to escalating episodes of violence within the institutional setting as a whole. Evidence has been found to suggest that at least 25 percent of incidents of inmate on inmate violence have homosexual underpinnings (Toch, 1965) and that homosexual activity may be the leading motive behind inmate homicides in American prisons (Sylvester, Reed, & Nelson, 1977; Nacci & Kane, 1983). If staff cannot be motivated to take an interest in minimizing sexual assault due to humanitarian pleas, these latter facts are usually sufficient for them to realize that the importance of preventing such acts is significant and has numerous ramifications for the safety of the inmates, the staff and the institution as a whole.

Besides educating staff and setting up a system whereby suspected cases of assault can be appropriately attended to and investigated, the institution psychologist may also have a responsibility to educate inmates on protecting themselves and identifying inmates at particular risk as part of the initial screening process. This would include providing information on how to receive help and basic information on avoiding accepting unsolicited "gifts" from other inmates or offers of protection. Inmates most likely to be targeted for assault include those who are younger, smaller, those with longer hair, those who discuss sex often with other inmates, those with effeminate mannerisms and those known or suspected to be homosexual (Nacci & Kane, 1984a,b). One might also suspect that those who are less sophisticated or "street smart" and less experienced in prison customs (e.g., first-time offenders) to also be at particular risk. Some inmates who meet the aforementioned characteristics may need to be seen privately to discuss how their appearance may make them more likely to be targets and to make them aware of situations they should be wary of in preventing themselves from being victimized.

As stated earlier, these duties do not typically require a great proportion of the psychologist's attention, however, in some cases the system can alert you to an inmate in need of crisis counseling as a result of assault or in need of special protection to avoid the virtual certainty of their being targeted. As an example of the latter case, this psychologist can offer one experience of a particular inmate who was assigned to the institution where I worked who met all of the criteria for making him likely to be targeted as a victim discussed above. The inmate was under 21 with a physical appearance and voice that made him seem to be between the ages of 14–16. He was sent to prison for vandalizing soda machines, a minor crime more common in young juveniles than hardened adult offenders. He had long hair, was rather effeminate in appearance and demeanor, had never served time in prison and was extremely naive. This individual was given a jail sentence of approximately one year as a "lesson" from a district judge who apparently had the intention of scaring him into avoiding further antisocial acts. What the judge probably did not realize, however, was that due to this inmate having a history of other juvenile crimes, borderline personality disorder and having "escaped" from a youth camp, he was sent to an institution that housed medium and high security offenders. His earlier escape had actually consisted of his hitchhiking from a youth camp to the State Capital with the intent of speaking to the Governor about some complaints he had. Most of the offenders within the institution were there for violent and/or repeat offenses, had prior experience being in prison, were older and had ten years or greater to serve on their sentences.

It was not hard to identify the inmate as "high risk." Counseling with him about the situation accomplished nothing, as he insisted in almost comical fashion that he was tough enough to handle himself. It was decided that the inmate would be housed in the isolation unit for his own protection while attempts were made to have him sent to a lower security environment. The inmate objected to the situation and became a constant source of irritation for many staff members with his constant, and usually trivial, demands. He had a high need for attention and great instability in mood and in his abilities to relate appropriately to staff members. After a period of approximately two months in which alternative housing arrangements could not be obtained and the inmate continued to insist on being released to the general population environment, it was decided (against psychological advice) that staff would comply with his wishes. The inmate was released to the compound on a Friday. That weekend an emergency call was made for psychological assistance. The inmate reported that he had been subjected to whistles, catcalls and propositions from nu-merous inmates on the compound. Additionally, one attempted to as-sault him sexually, but the inmate escaped. The stress from these events was apparently more than the inmate could handle. When the psychologist arrived he had been moved back into the isolation unit where he was curled up in the fetal position and unresponsive to those around him. At the time, the inmate did not complain about being placed back in the isolation unit, but within days he was requesting to return to general population.

At that time it was decided that, given the relatively brief nature of his sentence, his fragile psychoemotional adjustment and great susceptibility to being victimized further, that he would remain in the isolation unit until his release for his own protection. The inmate returned to court and was released early. The example shows how knowledge of risk factors can be effective in identifying an inmate for intervention and preventing sexual assaults. It should be noted that keeping the inmate on the isolation unit was not a popular idea with many of the correctional staff, some of whom felt he was receiving special treatment and should be left to fend for himself on the compound. However, the institution psychologist must take responsibility for ensuring the safety, humane treatment and prevention of assault whenever possible. The goals themselves are not unusual, but the manner in which the psychologist must accomplish them sometimes deviate from those of the other correctional staff. In the case described here, the inmate in question almost assuredly would have suffered great psychic harm were he to have been assaulted, given the already precarious nature of his mental functioning.

ENSURING THE HUMANE TREATMENT OF INMATES

Whether for moral reasons or purely to satisfy the dictates of the court, a common objective in all correctional institutions is to provide a humane and safe environment for the inmates incarcerated there. While cases of severe brutality are uncommon, more subtle problems can sometimes arise between inmates and staff due to the normal separation that tends to occur between these two populations. It is easy for staff members, who hear and read about the acts of criminality and aggression their charges have perpetrated daily and who are exposed to constant attempts to manipulate them, to become coldhearted and standoffish towards all inmates. They can come to see all of them as completely distrustful and manipulative and decide that the safest manner of dealing with them is to minimize all contact and refuse all requests. In the process, some legitimate inmate needs or requests may come to be denied without just cause.

Recognizing the difficulties of working in the correctional environment, it can sometimes be helpful to tactfully approach staff members and represent the inmates request with an opinion on it seeming to be a reasonable one to be taken under consideration. Mind you, it is not recommended that you intervene in this manner often and your individual relationship with the staff member in question may sometimes determine if you do it at all, but on occasion when the request appears to be one that may prevent problems and cause none, some quiet prodding can be in order. It is also recommended, as has been stated elsewhere in this book, to never indicate to an inmate that you are doing this or would ever be willing to do so, as this would be tantamount to hanging a "complaint department" sign on your office door. Inmates are notorious for complaining about anything and everything and for those of us with the advantage of freedom and countless choices every day, the minor complaints of inmates can often appear extremely trivial.

An example of a situation in which one may wish to intervene in matters best left to the correctional staff was my experience with one inmate with symptoms of PTSD resulting from involvement in the Vietnam War. The inmate had been an active treatment participant in both individual and group therapy, had always been a model inmate and never made any attempts at manipulation. His PTSD symptoms were largely controlled, with the exception of occasional flare-ups which would involve difficulty sleeping and a worsening of symptoms if the sleep disturbance continued. He was preparing to finish his sentence and go home when he was given a new cellmate that happened to be a prolific snorer. The inmate was having some increase in symptoms as his release date approached, but began looking noticeably tired and distressed with the addition of his new cellmate.

As a good psychologist, I greeted his initial complaints with some incredulity. Perhaps he did not like the new cellmate. Perhaps he was being threatened. Further exploration revealed that both inmates and staff on the unit were well aware of the cellmate's snoring "problem," which created complaints not only from those he shared a cell with, but also those who were housed in adjacent cells. Though I think it ill-advised to intervene into housing assignments, this particular situation seemed to call for it. Though I never claimed any credit to the inmate, I did intervene by strongly encouraging the unit staff to change his cell, particularly in light of his history of mental illness and sensitivity to sleep dysfunction.

The natural desire to not want to be manipulated by inmates and perhaps unconscious need to prove that one is not on their side so as to avoid the wrath of one's peers and/or an endless procession of inmates asking for favors can sometimes lead to irrational behavior on the staff's part that can be frustrating to work with. I can recall several instances of inmates who were a nuisance to members of the psychology department because of their general offensiveness and constant requests for services to which they are almost entirely unresponsive to. These inmates were often nuisances to the staff in charge of their housing units because of numerous disciplinary infractions. Whenever an additional infraction would occur, psychology staff would rejoice at the surety that the inmate would be transferred to an alternate, perhaps higher security, institution because of their inability to successfully adjust to their present environment, only to find out that the inmate would be retained. The reason often given by staff members? Because the inmate wanted to leave. If the inmate wants X, the feeling goes, give him Y. The obvious result of this only punishing the staff (myself included) rather than the inmate is usually lost on the staff determined to punish this inmate. Also lost, very often, is the realization that many inmates quickly learn this game and therefore request the opposite of their true desires. The resulting interactions can be quite humorous were they not so frustrating.

Another example of the struggle for power and control that can occur between staff and inmates that is somewhat more unusual is the case of an inmate who came into a minimum security institution and almost immediately complained of anxiety and insomnia as a result of being in crowded situations. The institution he was in housed the inmates in large dorms that were subdivided into four-bed cubicles. He indicated that he had always been a bit of a loner and was made terribly anxious by the degree of noise and activity of so many people in such a large, but confined, area. After repeated contacts in which he displayed no recognizable outer signs of the symptoms he reported and reported having obtained little benefit from medication, a harder line was taken with the inmate of his need to accept his situation and adjust accordingly. The inmate inquired as to what would happen if he engaged in prohibited actions and got locked up in solitary confinement. He then further asked if he could "check in" to such confinement without having to commit a prohibited act. The inmate was advised that he could be allowed for mental health reasons to be placed in confinement for a brief period, but that in so doing he risked being transferred to a higher security institution based on his lack of mental stability. As he was currently placed close to home and valued his family visits, he reconsidered and decided against pursuing his request.

Several weeks later information was given that the same inmate was being threatened by another inmate and both were placed in solitary confinement while an investigation could be conducted. The original inmate was found to be in no danger and was ordered to be returned to the general population. At this point, he stated that he still felt threatened and refused to leave his solitary cell. The result was a disciplinary write-up that resulted in his being punished by being ordered to remain in solitary confinement for 30 days. The inmate was unperturbed, and actually was noted to be quite comfortable in his new confines. After 30 days passed the same thing reoccurred. At this point it became obvious the inmate was not going to come out. Ordinarily, this would result in a transfer to a higher security institution, but it was decided that the inmate would instead be retained for as long as a year or more and kept in solitary confinement before transferring him as a way to teach him a lesson.

My observations that the inmate was quite content staying where he was were dismissed by staff members who did not have the ability to comprehend that anyone could actually enjoy solitary confinement. So in this case, an attempt to do what the inmate least wanted resulted in want he most wanted. As stated previously, the games that occur between staff and inmates in their struggle to exercise power over each other can be humorous were they not so frustrating. In the absence of egregious infringements on providing a humane setting for inmates, such events must sometimes be tolerated. After all, no bureaucracy works with complete rationality.

Regardless of idiosyncrasies that may arise from the unusual atmosphere of the prison environment, the criminal justice mentality and the bureaucratic nature of the system, the psychologist working within the system is perhaps uniquely able to see situations from a slightly different perspective which can be useful in maintaining an orderly and safe institutional environment, as well as an ultimately more pleasant atmosphere for all concerned. The psychologist's perspective is more likely to be able to encompass the likely long-term consequences of different actions by staff on the individual staff and inmate involved, in addition to the larger community of staff and inmates within the prison. Our input may not only be useful at times to front-line workers and/or administrative staff, but we would probably be negligent to withhold such information. Regardless of how it may or may not be utilized, our expertise in human behavior makes us morally obligated to offer our professional opinions on occasion. If this advice is particularly significant, placing the opinions in writing may offer one greater self-protection and also greater notice from administrators who may be more used to working within a bureaucratic system and, thus, to occasionally discount verbal input.

CRISIS INTERVENTIONS

Handling crisis contacts within a prison environment can oftentimes be quite similar to handling difficult issues in a manner that they would be encountered in any other type of setting. Regardless of where you work as a psychologist, individuals suffering from acute depression and anxiety are commonly encountered. Through supportive interventions, behavioral skills training, referral for medication and other common methods, many difficulties can be alleviated to tolerable levels. The motivations for these contacts are also common:

deaths in the family, personal illness, relationship difficulties, identity issues, and so forth.

In some situations, however, your crisis interventions will be more unique to the correctional environment. Inmates with anger management and impulse control problems will act out in what appear irrational ways, but are more a function of their lack of effective social and coping skills, than their inability to make rational decisions. Some inmates, particularly those who are younger and possess some borderline tendencies, can occasionally act out in ways best characterized as temper tantrums. An inmate, frustrated by not being given something he wants or for being punished for his own misbehavior by being given time in solitary confinement, may cut himself or threaten to commit suicide as a way of venting his inner emotional turmoil and attempting to manipulate the system. Some inmates believe if they act crazy enough they will be released from taking responsibility for their behavior, given milder punishment or granted the demands they seek (e.g., transfer to different cell, institution, or given new cellmate).

Their attempts to act irrationally usually succeed in getting them referred to the institution psychologist who may be relied on by correctional staff to bring the inmates under control. Although normal correctional procedures are the best method of dealing with these individuals, care needs to be taken for two primary reasons. First, the inmate is acting unstable and demonstrating his impulsivity. If treated too harshly and/or ignored too greatly, he may interpret the psychologists actions as a "dare" and increase the severity level of his actions by making a suicidal gesture. Second, the staff may be convinced of the inmate having a mental illness and be reluctant to treat him as a standard disciplinary case.

One common solution is to apply correctional techniques of isolation, direct observation, placing the inmate in a hard cell where he lacks most of the tools to commit self-harm, and/or putting the inmate in ambulatory or four-point restraints. The reasoning for taking this action may be explained to the inmate as being carried out to ensure his own safety and can be presented as part of a "confrontation avoidance" procedure with the inmate. That is, a period of trying to rationally discuss and work out a solution to the inmate's problem that can avoid more physically intense interventions such as forced cell moves. The purpose of confrontation avoidance is to minimize the risk of staff and inmate injuries. Discussing the correctional procedures that will take place in the absence of a change in the inmate's behavior as being done to ensure his safety implies an acceptance of the inmates personal distress while still attempting to bring his behavior under control. The inmates should also be informed that the conditions applied can be removed or even avoided if and when they are able to demonstrate an improved ability to control themselves and speak with you rationally. Handling the situation in this way allows the psychologist to help the inmates calm down without resorting to accusations of their malingering or of being too "crazy" to be able to control themselves, thus often working in cases of both mentally ill and personality disordered inmates.

As the inmate was initially engaging in a "temper tantrum" to get his way, the response to the procedures described usually go in one of two directions. Some inmates will immediately calm down and express a desire to talk in an effort to avoid the more punitive measures. Others will intensify and can easily remind you of a three-year-old child who swears to hold his breath until he is given what he requests. There are inmates that will yell and scream and engage in threats to harm themselves even when placed in four-point restraints. I believe at that point they are determined to prove they can outlast any punishment the staff is willing to try and believe they can eventually succeed in getting the staff to give in to their demands. The most persistent usually begin to soften their stance rather quickly and suddenly when their natural bodily functions begin to take on an increasing urgency, especially after a couple of hours when they may begin to feel the urge to devoid themselves of the contents of their colon and/or bladder. Their resolve to carry through their crusade melts with the more undesirable idea of having to relieve themselves without the advantages of a commode. Not only do the inmates tend to calm down at the time, but quite often they will cease to create a serious concern for the institution psychologist, instead returning to their normal routine.

This may be a difficult process for a psychologist to experience initially, as it is quite foreign to the more benign empathic procedures we studied so dutifully in graduate school. The powerful reinforcing effect of the inmates' submission and reintegration into the normal correctional routine, however, makes future episodes easier to undertake. Perhaps importantly also, the inmate has learned that prepubescent methods of dealing with parental-type authority will not likely serve him to the degree it may have in other settings.

PSYCHOTHERAPY

The large number and varied quality of responsibilities of the correctional psychologist, coupled with the unpredictability of the timing and amount of crises to occur at any given time, make the scheduling of regular individual and group sessions challenging. Additionally, many inmates have no interest in personality change, others don't trust any institutional employees and still others do not want to be associated with the psychology department to avoid being labeled as "crazy" by others. As a result, the actual time commitment spent in intensive, traditional forms of individual therapy is relatively small. Individual contacts are usually confined to dealing with immediate crises and getting the inmate adjusted or readjusted to the institutional environment at which time contacts are gradually stopped. Many inmates are willing to see the psychologist when in great personal distress to unload their emotions, but even then are often uninterested in engaging in major personal introspection. This becomes increasingly true as one progresses to the higher security levels. As a result, those in most need of treatment and, arguably, the best able to benefit from it, also tend to be the least interested.

Group interventions, if therapeutic in nature, bring on the added complication of placing a collection of paranoid individuals together with the proposed intention of building a trusting group able to share their inner emotions. The strong levels of defensiveness in most inmates ensure that the primary emotion shared will be anger and constructive dialogue will be kept to a minimum. In fact, they are probably more apt to reinforce each other's negativism and criminal attitudes. To be successful, therapeutic groups will often need to be highly structured with strict rules against diverting to common, but insig-nificant, complaint sessions. Psychoeducational groups are often more successful in this environment and given the relative lack of empathy and insight in the target population probably more useful.

I have found groups that discuss such topics as anger management and smoking cessation to be well attended, much needed and enthusiastically enjoyed by the inmate population. In fact, after having delivered groups to a diverse range of different populations, I must admit that inmates are amongst the best participants I have experienced in such groups. They will often ask quite intelligent and sometimes penetrating questions, the answers to which they sometimes don't like but usually are willing to listen to. The group situation gives them chances to ask questions about hypothetical others and receive answers to questions they have about themselves in a non-threatening and non-personal manner. I believe this to be an effective means for increasing insight into a group of individuals that is often frustrating to reach. It is important in the process of any group to give frequent concrete examples of concepts discussed and to be willing to spend as much time as the inmates desire answering questions and considering the points they bring up, for these are usually what allows them to see the personal relevance of what is being discussed so that they can truly benefit from the overall group content. In addition, I have also found psychoeducational groups to be a good way of building rapport and respect amongst the inmate population. It can further serve as an opportunity for an inmate to seek more individual attention before, after or between groups without having to break down and admit they need services from you.

PSYCHOACTIVE MEDICATIONS

Although prescription privileges remain elusive, psychologists working in corrections are typically involved as central figures in the prescribing and monitoring of psychotropics. Most institutions do not have a resident psychiatrist, so the task of prescribing medications for psychiatric complaints often falls upon a consulting psychiatrist who makes occasional and brief visits or on the general medical doctor at the institution. In either case, the role of the psychologist in deciding who receives medications is often primary. Consulting psychiatrists typically must rely on the psychologists report of inmates behavior and institutional functioning since their own contact with inmates is rather brief and superficial. The psychologist often functions as the "gatekeeper" who decides which inmates are allowed to see the psychiatrist and then provides necessary background information and a brief assessment of the inmate so the psychiatrist can make an informed decision regarding treatment.

It is often the case that consulting psychiatrists will come from outside the correctional system altogether and have little knowledge or understanding of the special nature of the patients they are evaluating. The psychiatrist, like most others, will be unlikely to have encountered the degree of malingering, manipulation and deceptive practices routinely encountered in the inmate population. In these cases, the psychologist should be prepared to brief the psychiatrist on suspected manipulation before the interview occurs and follow the interview with any pertinent information they may have, such as the lack of correspon dence between the inmates reports on that day versus previous contacts. In the case where the general medical doctor also provides psychotropic medication, the psychologist should not assume the doctor is capable of effective screening and diagnosis, nor well-versed in psychopharmacology. It is not unusual for the doctor to heavily rely on the psychologist for not only affirmative or preliminary diagnoses, but for suggestions on appropriate medications. In some cases, even dosage recommendations are appreciated.

Even when a consulting psychiatrist is the dispensing physician, it remains important for the psychologist to have some training in psychopharmacology. This is particularly significant in regards to knowledge of the undesirable side effects of these medications because the role of monitoring and suggesting discontinuation or alteration of medications is almost always the primary task of the psychologist. It is wise to work out a system in advance with consulting psychiatrists for them to authorize medication adjustments in the face of needed changes in their absence. In some cases, this might involve writing an order outlining backup medication recommendations in the event of significant side effects or authorizing increased dosages of a set degree if therapeutic benefits are not achieved within a set period of time.

It is a good idea to utilize your role as the primary gatekeeper of psychotropic medications to minimize their presence within the institution. When medication becomes too easy to obtain, additional time and energy will be required to deal with inmates malingering symptoms of mental illness in an effort to obtain mood-altering drugs. Regardless of who is the prescribing authority you should use whatever influence you have to minimize, if not abolish, the use of addictive medications with a high potential for abuse. This would include the benzodiazepines, barbituates, and Ritalin®. In addition, although still not regarded as addictive, the presence of Prozac® as a street drug attests to its potential for abuse and addiction and its interactive effects with alcohol make it an attractive mind-altering chemical amongst inmate populations. Given the many alternative tricyclics, Prozac should probably not be regarded as the preferred medication for depression within an institutional environment. Seroquel is another medication that has become well-known amongst inmates for it desirable mind-altering effects. It is necessary when working in a prison to be vigilant about any medications that are specifically requested by inmates or for which repeated requests are received for increases in dosage. It should never be assumed that any psychotropic medication is free of a potential for abuse, as there are some inmates who will happily abuse any substance with mind-altering effects. It should never be assumed that because you are dealing with prison inmates that they will not be using illicit drugs or alcohol in concert with any prescribed medications. In the present day, there are no entirely drug-free environments.

As in any environment in which psychologists perform their professional duties, one's level of rapport and ability to cooperatively coordinate with whatever M.D. prescribes medications for mental illness can greatly influence the degree of difficulty one experiences on the job. A competent and cooperative M.D. can make life a great deal easier, so taking efforts to establish and nurture this relationship is always wise. It is most difficult to be in a position of administering to the day-to-day needs of inmates when medications prescribed by an outsider do not coincide with your more informed clinical judgements. In these situations, the psychologist is often forced to reap what the psychiatrist sowed. For example, when there is clear overuse of medications within a facility, or evidence of particular inmates occurring that are abusing their medications, when there is no psychiatrist on site, it is usually the psychologist who is regarded as responsible, if not negligent. This perception can be applied even when the psychologist voiced disagreement with the specific writing of a prescription or the general pattern in which they were given in the institution. Given the primary role psychologists in most institutions have for management of the mentally ill, it is always a wise psychologist who involves themself with screening out inmates who clearly do not need medications before they see a psychiatrist and who makes every effort to keep their use minimized and appropriate. As progress is made in future years in obtaining prescription privileges for specially trained psychologists, the correctional field should be an ideal locale to integrate these new specialists. The benefits would appear to be considerable, both in the coordination of patient care for the inmate, the lack of duplication of efforts, and the elimination of unnecessary costs for institutions unable to afford full-time psychiatrists on site.

FORENSIC WORK

Working within a forensic assignment in the correctional field presents its own unique challenges and experiences. Several excellent sources of material exist which describe some of the major issues of performing assessments, administering expert testimony and discussing some of the major issues of forensic practice (Brodsky, 1991; Melton, Petrila, Poythress, & Slobogin, 1997; Tsushima & Anderson, 1996). Chapters 5 and 6 discuss the detection of malingering and deception through clinical interviews and psychological assessment that is crucial knowledge for anyone doing work in the correctional field. To get further into this area, however, is to open a Pandora's box that goes beyond the scope of the present book. It is important to realize that regardless of whether one is focused primarily on forensics or works on it in a purely ancillary basis, as a correctional psychologist you can be reasonably assured that you will be called on to perform evaluations of various issues for the courts.

Rather than being intimidated by the specter of being grilled on the witness stand by an aggressive attorney, this is better viewed as an opportunity to acquire experience in assessment with some of the most interesting types of assessment cases the field of psychology has to offer. It is actually the rare case that necessitates a trip to court and an appearance on the witness stand, and an even rarer case to be faced with a hostile reception by the court. However, even in the most difficult cases, adequate preparation, a cool head, a straightforward understandable delivery of testimony (much like the way you might teach an introductory psychology course), and avoidance of succumbing to irrational inner anxieties should be sufficient to perform well. Additionally, involvement in this work can easily serve to stimulate and motivate you towards professional development in the assessment arena.

The field of forensic psychology is a growing one that offers many rewards for private practice (without involvement in the morass of managed care) either while simultaneously working in the correctional field or in the future. As a correctional psychologist you will have an opportunity to assess challenging cases that are sure to hone your assessment skills. This can be used as an opportunity to develop skills that can be used in a private practice setting on a part-time basis or upon terminating one's employment with the correctional system involved.

DRUG TREATMENT

Included in the United States government's proclaimed war on drugs has been an increasing emphasis on drug treatment programs at many levels. There is no denying that drugs are a major contributor to illegal activities in the United States. At all levels of the drug distribution hierarchy are individuals who commit increasing numbers of property and violent crimes as a means of continuing their drug habit. In addition to punishing their criminal conduct with prison sentences, it would seem necessary to abolish their dependence on illicit drugs in order to enable them to carry on a lifestyle devoid of continued illegalities. In keeping with this reasoning, drug education and drug treatment programs have sprung up in virtually all states and within the Federal Prison System as well. The quality and comprehensiveness of these programs varies considerably. At one end of the spectrum are intensive, multifaceted, programs led by clinical psychologists that address all aspects of dependency in a systematic and contemporary manner. An example of such programs are those in place with the Federal System that have been described in the literature in detail (Hayes, 1993). At the other end of the spectrum are some state and county programs that consist of relatively untrained and unsupervised treatment providers that may lead largely unsubstantial 12-step type groups or other similar activity. In some prisons, in fact, drug treatment may consist of a non-professional inserting a videotape on drugs with no effort to coordinate any discussion or evaluation of their content. It is an unfortunate fact that some systems are more interested in being able to claim they provide some type of treatment than they are in actually providing treatment of any useful value.

It is an unfortunate consequence of limited funding brought on by increasing prison populations and decreasingly willingness to correspondingly expand their expenditures that previously impressive programs in State and Federal institutions have deteriorated in quantity and quality in recent years. Many State programs have ceased providing treatment at all. Federal institutions have largely eliminated programming, with the exception of drug treatment. Unfortunately, in that system drug treatment is used to shorten inmate sentences, so an effort has been made to expand greatly the number of inmates served to help relieve population pressures. The quality of programming and the level of staffing has simultaneously fallen precipitously as funds have become more scarce. This mimics previous similar circumstances in public agencies such as the U.S. Department of Veterans Affairs where quality programs of the past often succumbed to inadequate financial commitment from government sources in Washington, D.C. The single contrast to this trend in providing quality treatment that continues to obtain fashionable increases in funding appears to reside in outpatient community drug diversion programs working in concert with drug courts. Those psychologists interested in coordinating drug treatment in a personally and professionally satisfying environment are advised to explore this area of opportunity.

Given the wide disparity in the quality of drug programs, it may be difficult to accurately measure the effectiveness of such interventions. Actually, it is quite astounding given the number and types of treatments now available how little published research exists that has attempted to assess the usefulness of such efforts. The research that does exist suggests that this type of treatment is both useful and cost-effective. Field (1989) found that addicted offenders with little or no treatment while incarcerated displayed an accelerating pattern of criminal activity over time. Matched participants who participated in a comprehensive drug dependency treatment program on an inpatient basis showed reduced numbers of arrests, convictions and incarcerations. Additionally, longer treatment (12 months) was found to be more effective than more time-limited interventions.

Chance et al. (1990) evaluated a treatment program for drug and alcohol addicted inmates in a medium security prison based on reality therapy and control theory. The program was focused on recognizing inappropriate behaviors and learning new socially valued skills. When compared to non-treated controls, program participants were seen at the end of treatment as possessing more positive attitudes towards themselves, the program and others whether being evaluated by staff or through self-reports.

Rouse (1991) reviewed the available literature on drug treatment programs and concluded that they provided cheap, cost-effective, interventions when operated within existing prisons. It was noted that programs tended to show more positive effects when operated within the prison setting rather than in halfway houses. Recidivism rates for program participants were found to be at least 10 percent lower than those of controls. Considering the low cost of providing treatment and the engagement of inmates in prosocial activities that may serve to reduce problems within institutions while the inmates are involved in treatment, the gains appear quite worthwhile. Future research focusing on the most organized programs may well demonstrate even more substantial benefits. This is not to suggest that all inmates, regardless of crime and history, should be subjected to these interventions, however. Major (1992) shows that drug treatment is not effective when it wasn't matched to inmates' needs and desires for treatment.

The United States Federal Bureau of Prisons recently released a preliminary study of the outcomes of inmates who participated in a comprehensive 500-hour residential drug treatment program while incarcerated (U.S. Department of Justice, 1998). Inmates were examined during the first six months following their release from custody. Those inmates who completed drug treatment were 73 percent less likely to be rearrested and 44 percent less likely to have used drugs during their first six months of release. Subsequent longer-term outcome studies demonstrated far more modest beneficial effects (and received far more modest publicity). Nevertheless, such positive initial results suggest that treatment offers a significant window of opportunity that could likely be extended further if releasing inmates could be appropriately routed to positive community after-care programs and/or placed in suitable employment opportunities upon release. The Federal system has largely failed to address such crucial components of treatment.

Evidence in support of such ideas is demonstrated in a study of 478 prisoners in the California State System in which it was found that after three years, only 27 percent of inmate's involved in the prison's drug treatment program with aftercare returned to prison, compared to a recidivism rate of 75 percent for those not involved in the program (Wexler et al., 1999).

Similar success was demonstrated in the State of Delaware which featured a program in which some inmates transitioned back into the community through a work-release program involving therapeutic communities-drug free residential settings which provided continuous monitoring by counselors, group therapy and family sessions. After three years those involved with the program had significantly less drug use and rearrests than those who did not complete the program (Martin et al., 1999).

It is likely that psychologists will play an active role in the continuing development of drug programs of increasing quality and also will be instrumental in systematically evaluating what components most significantly increase the overall effectiveness of treatment programs and what types of participants have the greatest likelihood of demonstrating treatment gains. In the field of corrections, the ability to track participants' progress after completing treatment through probation and criminal records gives one a unique opportunity to measure treatment effectiveness. In fact, the field of corrections may well possess the best ability to effectively carry out research measuring program effectiveness in the drug treatment field because of the inherent difficulties following up on participants in non-correctional programs. Achieving such gains will require a greater and more consistent commitment to adequately funding such endeavors, however.

SEXUAL OFFENDER TREATMENT

The majority of treatment programs for sexual offenders are directed by psychologists and most of these are housed within a correctional facility. Treatment efforts vary considerably, but traditionally have involved some type of behavioral sexual arousal retraining and group therapy. More progressive approaches have begun using cognitive behavioral methods and/or relapse prevention techniques. Additionally, castration, either physical or chemical, has been an historical treatment that has retained some popular appeal. Each of these will be discussed.

Use of Castration

The appeal of castrating sexual offenders is in the swiftness, direct relation of the punishment to the crime, rational belief that it should be effective and belief that the problem emanates from an overproductive sexual drive. The former two reasons are hard to argue against, but the validity of the latter two arguments is highly questionable. Research has shown that at least 10 percent of castrates continue to have erections (Brown & Courtis, 1977). In fact, in some cases an actual increase in sexual activity following the procedure has resulted (Heim, 1981). Moreover, as the press for more seemingly civilized and humane treatments have become more emphasized in our society, physical castrations have largely been replaced by suggestions of utilizing chemical means of castration.

Two drugs, cyproterone acetate (Androcur) and medroxyprogesterone (Provera), have been shown to reduce androgen levels and sex drive. The drugs are hormonal analogues that act as androgenic antagonists that compete for sites of action both in the central nervous system and peripherally for which androgens have an affinity (Bradford, 1990). Their effectiveness with sexual offenders remains quite questionable. Marshall et al. (1991), in a review of such studies, concluded that the medications have not consistently demonstrated the ability to produce reductions in deviant sexual thoughts or masturbation rates, two behaviors rationally related to the criterion behavior. Cooper (1987) shows that MPA, even when demonstrated to reduce testosterone, does not always demonstrate a reduction in deviant sexual arousal. He concluded that once sexual arousal is established, it may become independent of testosterone levels which may fall to zero without influencing sexual responsiveness. Thus, there may be some argument for using the drugs in concert with other established treatments, but there appears little support for using them in isolation.

Behavioral Treatment

Sexual arousal retraining using a classical conditioning model has been a standard treatment procedure for sexual offenders for several decades. The most widely used approach was pioneered by Freund (1965) and involves the use of a penile plethysmograph. The device measures penile tumescence while the subject is exposed to appropriate and inappropriate sexually arousing stimuli. Reactions to the various stimuli is directly assessed with the treatment goal of reducing inappropriate arousal while maintaining or improving appropriate arousal. Thus, the subject may view slides of nude children, nude adults and neutral stimuli. Furthermore, when exposed to the child slides, they may be exposed to a noxious stimulus (e.g., ammonia salts) designed to reduce any inappropriate arousal.

This method is not without problems. First, it is known that erections can be brought under conscious control (Quinsey & Chaplin, 1988) and that the problem is most significant amongst offenders who deny that they have a problem (Freund & Watson, 1991). This implies that a particularly antisocial, and perhaps dangerous, offender could manipulate their way through this type of treatment program with no actual change in arousal, thought or behavior patterns. Second, the method assumes that sexual arousal retraining as measured in the laboratory will generalize to real-world settings. It would appear suspect to merely assume that such a powerful biological drive would be expected to be transformed in real-life from viewing pictures in a treatment room. Regardless of whether erections were being manipulated or not, the absence of discriminative stimuli to signal the likelihood of punishment for inappropriate arousal in the real environment would seem to minimize generalization. Finally, the method assumes a close correlation between sexual arousal and sexual offending. The actual motivation of the sexual offender, however, may not be sexual at all in many cases (Prendergast, 1991; Murphy & Peters, 1992; Hanson et al., 1991; Blader & Marshall, 1989).

Cognitive Interventions

For any treatment to be effective it would appear logical that the subject themselves must accept that they have a problem and possess a genuine desire to have it treated. As outlined above, behavioral methods are likely to be subject to manipulation and castration may have little effect whatsoever. More recent treatment efforts have incorporated elements of the relapse prevention model (Marlatt & Gordon, 1985), and other skill-building techniques to treat sexual offenders, usually in concert with traditional behavioral techniques.

Maletzky (1991) outlined a multifaceted treatment program in the State of Oregon. There treatment consists of behavioral interventions to retrain sexual arousal patterns, social skills training, orgasmic reconditioning and other interventions. An analysis of 3,800 offenders who completed the program and were released for periods of one to 17 years resulted in an impressive treatment success rate of 91 percent. Marques and Nelson (1992) have outlined a relapse prevention program for incarcerated sexual offenders that shows promise of increasing the effectiveness of traditional programming as well.

Treatment Effectiveness

Malcolm, Andrews and Quinsey (1993) demonstrated the usefulness of retaining phallometric measures in the treatment of sexual offenders. Their study showed clear correlations between male erectile responses and the similarity of sexual stimuli to the offender's most recent victim. Additionally, level of phallometrically measured responses was found to be predictive of recidivism rates. The authors reported an overall recidivism rate of 14 percent for treated offenders over an average 4.2 year follow-up interval. Other studies have also demonstrated the predictive validity of phallometric assessments for child molesters in both short-term (Marshall & Barbaree, 1990) and long-term (Malcolm, Andrews & Quinsey 1993; Rice, Quinsey & Harris, 1991) follow-ups. The addition of data regarding level of psychopathy from the PCL-R (Hare, 1991) appears to add additional predictive capacity (Rice, Harris, & Quinsey, 1990). The ability of phallometric assessment to predict outcome does not seem to generalize to incest offenders (Quinsey, Chaplin & Carrigan, 1979), and its ability to predict outcomes for rapists remains controversial (Blader & Marshall, 1989).

Rice, Quinsey and Harris (1991) examined the recidivism rates of 136 child molesters who received traditional behavioral interventions. Results show that treatment did not have any effect on recidivism rates. The apparent ineffectiveness of the treatment in this case may have been due to its limited scope, involvement of maximum security patients and absence of aftercare. Pithers (1990) has outlined a relapse prevention program for sexual offenders that demonstrated an impressively small 4 percent relapse rate over a 5-year period with 147 pedophiles.

The literature as a whole is quite inconsistent in the level of effectiveness of treatment programs and in the types of offenders most effectively treated (Bradford, 1990). The disparity of outcomes is troubling and should be a legitimate avenue of exploration in future studies to determine the specific factors involved in treatment effectiveness. Clearly, greater collaboration and coordination is needed across programs for greater effectiveness and consistency of results. There also appears to be a consistent percentage of offenders that are unresponsive to treatment across all programs. There is, as yet, no reliable data to allow selection of those who will or will not benefit from treatment intervention. It may be possible through further research to identify those most likely to be resistant to intervention such that program effectiveness and efficiency can be increased from current levels. At this point the inclusion of the PCL-R in screening potential participants would seem wise given some evidence of its ability to predict responsiveness to treatment (Rice, Harris & Quinsey, 1990).

Treatment effectiveness in this area is difficult to surmise in that the main factor determining effectiveness is likely to be inner motivation.

While it may be hard to imagine successfully participating in the more intensive confrontation-oriented groups included in some treatment programs without a sincere desire for change occurring at some point, with antisocials this is always a concern. Unfortunately, accurate measurement of one's true motivation for behavior and cognitive change and the extent to which such change occurs over time is inherently impossible to measure. Outcome measures, such as recidivism, are likely to significantly underestimate the number who reoffend as both the percentage of cases that come to the attention of law enforcement and those that are successfully prosecuted represents a relatively small number of the actual incidents which occur. Compounding the problem is the relatively low rate of recidivism even amongst untreated offenders, which often runs around 15 percent, thus making it difficult to demonstrate a measurable impact (Hanson et al., 2002). Still, the results available in the literature confirm that the best programs provide a measurable positive impact on participants that would argue for continued efforts to provide and improve treatment offerings.

Recently in the *State of Kansas vs. Hendricks*, the United States Supreme Court ruled that inmates can legally be detained in mental institutions against their will after the completion of their criminal sentences when it is determined that they still represent a significant predatory threat to the community (U.S. Supreme Court, 1997). This decision, coupled with many states increasing sentences for such crimes to life or near life and community notification laws that make reentrance into the community difficult for convicted sexual offenders call into question the future of treatment for sexual offenders. In 2006, President Bush signed into law the Adam Walsh Child Protection and Safety Act (PL 109-248) which formalized a Federal system for monitoring sexual offenders after their release and allowed for the indefinite detention at the Federal level of convicted sexual offenders that are deemed to represent a continued threat to the community should they be released. This might be regarded as a noble effort were we able to reliably identify such a sub-class of sexual offenders.

The difficulty in justifying continued treatment efforts is compounded by the high degree of publicity that any treatment failure receives and the public's extreme intolerance for this particular type of offender. Even if a program is overwhelmingly successful, for example, a single high publicity treatment failure can doom efforts to maintain the funding necessary for continuation of treatment programs. Finally, psychologists working in this field should recognize that they are unlikely to achieve great acceptance by the public or even their own colleagues. Proper recognition, even for programs of high quality, are not likely to be forthcoming, which may negatively influence the ability of this area of work to attract and retain enough high quality motivated professionals to see it continue to progress.

The typical institution will not, of course, tend to contain a full-scale treatment program for sex offenders. In systems in which such programs exist, they will usually have some preferences on techniques for the institutional psychologist to use to prepare the inmate prior to their transfer into the institution that houses the program. The more typical example is probably that of the psychologist functioning in a system that lacks any available treatment program for sexual offenders. In this climate, one is probably best served by providing individual and/or group therapy using a relapse prevention model, orgasmic reconditioning and perhaps other elements of treatment identified in initial interviews as needed. There is little evidence to suggest that the more expensive treatment devices, such as plethysmographs, provide any demonstrably greater outcome than these more cost-effective and simpler techniques.

BOOT CAMPS

Development of military-style boot camps within the Nation's prison systems blossomed in the 1980s and 1990s in response to the popular view that many offenders are young males that lack the self-discipline necessary to live within socially accepted lifestyle parameters. By focusing on instilling military discipline, self-responsibility and an appreciation of hard work, it is hoped that a greater appreciation for societal mores will result. Additionally, such "treatment" satisfies our psychological need for retribution by making inmates work hard and appear to suffer somewhat, rather than be pampered by a prison environment that is too forgiving of them. Boot camps are frequently administered by psychologists which may assist in having it qualify as rehabilitative in nature, but also is likely to help prevent the "tough conditions" from deviating from humane procedures.

The inherently positive view the public has of the goals and procedures of boot camps have not been lost on our nation's politicians. A program that began in 1983 in the states of Georgia and Oklahoma had grown to encompass at least 46 boot camps in 31 different states by the end of 1993 (MacKenzie, 1993). United States President Clinton's 1994 crime bill earmarked $3 billion for the development of additional camps. At the beginning of 1995, 75 boot camps were in operation within United States state and federal prisons (Camp & Camp, 1995). It is unfortunate that this type of popularity occurred without sufficient research data to back up the effectiveness of such programs. After the mid-1990s, the number of boot camps declined. By 2000, nearly one-third of State prison boot camps had closed (Camp & Camp, 2001).

Few research studies could be located that systematically looked at the effectiveness of prison boot camps. Burns and Vito (1994) performed an analysis of the boot camp program in the state of Alabama. They compared recidivism rates of boot camp graduates to those who were instead either granted probation or served a period of incarceration followed by probation. The nature of offenses and age of offenders were comparable across the three groups. Findings indicated that the camp graduates had slightly lower recidivism rates than those granted immediate probation, but had slightly higher recidivism rates when contrasted with those that received a period of incarceration. The differences between the three groups were rather small and not statistically significant. The authors concluded that the camps may help reduce prison costs by slightly lowering recidivism rates as compared to traditional incarceration if the camp participants serve a shorter period of time in the prison system. Given the small differences, though, it is hard to justify not merely giving them probation from the start, though the authors dodged this inference in an apparent attempt to salvage some degree of favorable results.

Corbett and Petersilia (1994) carried out a study of boot camps in eight states. Their finding was that the boot camps demonstrated no positive effect on recidivism rates or the participant's adjustment to the community. The only positive benefits that could be demonstrated from program participation was minor improvements to problems with prison crowding and in the attitudes of the participants at the conclusion of the program. The attitude changes shown include having more positive views of the future, their experiences, how they benefitted from their program participation and having less antisocial attitudes. It should be noted that the last of these, a decline in antisocial attitudes, was also noted in traditionally incarcerated offenders.

A comprehensive evaluation study in 2003 consistently showed that boot camps did not reduce recidivism regardless of whether the camps were for adults or juveniles or whether they were first-generation programs with a heavy military emphasis or later programs with more emphasis on treatment (National Institute of Justice, 2003).

The benefits of boot camps have not been demonstrated and their future in the prison system at this point is questionable. The positive view the public has and the resultant political benefits of supporting these programs may be sufficient for them to continue into the foreseeable future, though it appears that many of those that remain are becoming private operations geared towards juveniles which encourage parents with troubled youth to send their children for behavioral reprogramming. The research literature would suggest, however, that the monies spent on these programs in the prison system at least could more effectively be diverted to more focused rehabilitative efforts.

VALUES BASED PROGRAMS

The Federal Bureau of Prisons has recently launched new treatment initiatives designed to train inmates to accept greater personal responsibility for their behavior and develop basic interpersonal skills to allow them to respond in more appropriate and effective ways to their environmental and legal situations. The Beckley Responsibility and Values Enhancement (BRAVE) program was developed as a method of targeting criminologic belief systems in hopes of reducing inmate misconduct both within and beyond the prison setting. Particularly geared towards inmates of young age at the beginning of relatively long sentences, the program is designed in particular for inmates whose demographic characteristics (e.g., age, sentence length, offense, etc.) suggest that they are particularly likely to present disciplinary problems for the institution and/or more likely to participate in inmate group disturbances. The program lasts approximately nine months and includes treatment components focused on instilling pro-social values, communication skills, anger management, drug awareness, and identification of destructive cognitive processes. It also seeks to provide education in civics, peer pressures, as well as enhancing ones general physical and spiritual health. Completion requires participation in a "service" project to make amends to the community by means of making a positive social contribution. The Challenge, Opportunity, Discipline and Ethics (CODE) program is currently being implemented in United States Penitentiaries and is similarly designed to reduce inmate misbehavior and encourage more prosocial attitudes and skills.

Components of these programs are not novel and borrow heavily from previously established treatment programs in the Federal Bureau of Prisons, especially the Residential Drug Treatment Programs and programs on values exploration and development. Previous observations that Penitentiary inmates who participated in Residential Drug Treatment had half the number of disciplinary actions as those who did not led to an interest in broadening treatment to inmates who did not have drug problems or who were unwilling to admit to such. Both the BRAVE, CODE and Values programs were developed as a result.

These programs appear to have followed the principles set down by Andrews et al. (1990) in providing services that are targeted towards a specific need and focused on high risk offenders, who are most likely to benefit from treatment interventions. These programs and others like them represent attempts to provide contemporary applications of current knowledge in innovative efforts to provide rehabilitation while making prisons safer for all concerned. Unfortunately, they often are unfocused in application and the programs described herein appear to largely involve a softer version of the moralistic treatment approach of boot camps and early model sex offender programs. The early benefit demonstrated in research may be merely a function of higher staffing levels and attention given inmates in such programs and a comparison group would be helpful in separating out such possible effects in evaluating program effectiveness.

Unfortunately, bureaucratic organizations with fluctuating funding, changing leadership and somewhat unsophisticated administrators make it difficult to protect the integrity of any such attempts at comprehensive programs and all of these programs suffered or were terminated over time. The one's remaining have shown only modest positive impacts that are as likely related to increased staffing and attention to the inmate participants as to any programmatic components involved.

As such programs are attempted, results regarding treatment gains and safer institutional environments for both inmates and staff may be instrumental in determining if such programs will continue to expand in our nation's prison systems. However, careful construction of these programs and commitment to long-term development are crucial if they are to have a chance at success.

PET THERAPY

Although sparsely reported in the literature, there have been attempts to use pets to teach responsibility in inmates and reduce levels of aggression. Lee (1983) compared groups of criminally mentally ill inpatients that either were given or not given pets. Those given a pet to care for displayed a need for only half the levels of medication to control their illnesses as those without pets, and showed a significant decline in violence and suicide attempts as well.

Moneymaker and Strimple (1991) have described a program at the no closed Lorton Correctional Facility in Lorton, Virginia, in which vocational training in becoming a certified Assistant Laboratory Animal Technician is provided as an option to inmates. The training involves being assigned animals and being given responsibility for their care and maintenance. Participants in the program have shown increases in evaluations of their self-worth and a more positive outlook towards others. Behavioral demonstrations of their improvements have included participants being involved in fewer altercations and problem behaviors. The program serves an additional function of finding a home for animals otherwise destined for destruction.

A recent review of prison pet programs identified programs in thirty-six states and a total of 159 sites throughout the country (Furst, 2006). The most common design is the community service model in which animals are rehabilitated, often in cooperation with local animal shelters, and then adopted out to the community. Service animal socialization programs are the second most frequent type of program. In these, participants socialize and begin the training of puppies, which are then sent on to more advanced service animal training, such as dogs for the blind or drug detection. A majority of programs include an association with a local nonprofit organization that administers the program and provides the animals, supplies and training. The organizations include animal shelters, rescue groups, county hu-mane societies and service animal agencies. The most commonly cited benefit of such programs is the sense of responsibility instilled in participants from caring for a dependent animal.

Such efforts unite two neglected populations, inmates and homeless animals, in a relationship that appears to benefit both and can serve a positive benefit to the community as well. Some programs offer certification in one or more areas of animal care that can lead to job opportunities post-release. The unconditional positive regard received from an animal can be of particular significance to a prison inmate that is vulnerable to social isolation and lack of available financial support. An additional benefit of such programs is the positive community relations fostered by these type of programs (Harkrader, Burke & Owen, 2004) and the productive use of inmates time it provides.

Greater efforts to initiate programs of this type and to systematically evaluate existing programs will be necessary for informed decisions to be made as to whether this type of programming can be useful in reducing violence and instilling more positive attitudes in inmate participants. It would appear to represent a low-cost, high benefit, opportunity that could be relatively easily implemented across many prison institutions, however.

PERSONNEL SELECTION

For the most part, a psychologist's role in the employment selection process is not extensive. Owing to the hazards and stresses of the job, the fact that many prisons are located in remote geographic areas, the high turnover of correctional positions, and the elimination of candidates with negative historical backgrounds, there does not tend to be a large pool of candidates to choose from in filling employment positions. Moreover, those drawn to this type of work are probably more often interested in the greater activity and respect associated with employment as a traditional police officer rather than the more routine and neglected role of the correctional officer.

Psychologists will often have a role to play in the screening of correctional officer applicants. The actual function that the psychologist plays varies considerably depending on the correctional system you find yourself in, but usually is somewhat limited. In many cases, your role may be purely as an expert in performing rough screenings of the mental competency and ensuring a lack of significant mental illness of candidates. In these situations, few candidates are rejected and most would have likely been identified by non-experts during routine personnel screenings. It is often the psychologist's role to evaluate candidates who reveal that they have some history of treatment by psychologists or psychiatrists in their history. In these cases, one may conduct a more extensive private interview with the candidate to assess whether they can be reasonably expected to cope with the stresses and isolation associated with the role of being a correctional officer.

In some environments, the psychologist may be required or have the opportunity to administer standardized assessment instruments to assist in the screening of candidates. The most often utilized assessments in this regard are probably an abbreviated version of a standardized intelligence test and the MMPI. Published research on the selection of correctional officers is virtually absent, such that one will have to largely rely on standard interpretive strategies. Obviously, excessive suspiciousness, indications of psychosis and extreme impulsiveness would not be desirable traits in a correctional officer. As far as which traits to look for on the positive side, research leaves us few clues, probably owing to the diversity of such a large population of individuals. One study does offer a word of warning about the over-interpretation of the MMPI in this type of employment selection, however. Bowen (1985) compared the MMPI results of correctional officer and sheriff deputy candidates hired for employment. He found no significant differences between the two groups. Both were found to have a tendency to give guarded and defensive profiles with elevations on K, Ky, Pd and Ma common. An F-K greater than twelve and low scores on Si also were common. Knowing that individuals in this field tend to be more physically active and oriented, while less introspective is consistent with these results. The important idea for the evaluating psychologist to remember is to not try to make too much of defensive profiles, as the purpose of the MMPI is to assist in screening out grossly disturbed test-takers, not to identify some theoretically ideal candidate.

The Inwald Personality Inventory (Inwald, Knatz, & Shusman, 1982) was designed to assist in the screening and selection of correctional officer candidates. The IPI consists of 26 scales designed to measure stress reactions and deviant behavior patterns by focusing on absence and lateness problems, alcohol and drug use and antisocial behaviors. Shusman, Inwald and Landa (1984) provided some confirmatory evidence for the use of the IPI in the selection of correctional officer candidates. In their analysis, IPI results were able to accurately classify 73 percent of 716 male correctional officers as to whether they were ultimately retained or terminated after hiring. MMPI results on the same subjects resulted in an accuracy rate of 63 percent. Although the study suggests some utility to testing, the large percentage of candidates misclassified further suggests that psychological test results should be used in a conservative manner, primarily for the identification of gross difficulties.

HOSTAGE NEGOTIATION

The correctional environment is marked by occasional management difficulties owing to the nature of the population it involves. Hostage situations, while uncommon, must be anticipated to occur and prepared for in advance to ensure the highest probability of their being successfully resolved. The institution psychologist is in a natural position to offer guidance and assistance to any such effort given their expertise in human behavior and mental illness. The psychologist should probably have some preparation to perform as the primary negotiator though one's experience in handling difficult and aggressive inmates and other patients provides some relevant experience in dealing with the emotionally charged situation where hostages are taken. If the psychologist is not in the primary negotiating role, their expertise may still be crucial in providing suggestions and opinions to the negotiator on the psychological state of the hostage-taker and resultant methods of interaction most likely to offer success in resolving the situation. Of course, the psychologist may also be best able to offer insights gleaned from previous contacts with the individual inmate and/or interpret their past social history for assessments of their risk level and points of discussion most likely to be successful for the development of rapport between the negotiator and hostage-taker.

In addition to assistance, the psychologist may offer within a hostage situation itself, the psychologist can also be crucial in educating staff members and hostage negotiation team members on mentally preparing themselves for such events. Through role playing and behavioral practice, the psychologist may be able to offer feedback to negotiation team members on managing stress in critical situations that could be crucial in an actual emergency. The psychologist could also discuss with all staff members how to handle being taken hostage in such a manner that maximizes the hostage's ability to survive the situation both physically and mentally. Training of this nature would present a good opportunity to discuss symptoms of PTSD and the best strategies for dealing with such problems in the acute stage when resolvement of emotional turmoil is most likely to be effective. Discussion of the Stockholm syndrome (Ochberg, 1980; Strentz, 1982) that the hostages' experience could also lessen feelings of confusion and anxiety staff members may have should they become involved in long-term situations and prepare negotiators and observing staff for what might otherwise be interpreted as irrational or unprofessional behavior.

FAMILY AND EMPLOYEE CRISIS ASSISTANCE

Following a major institutional disturbance, hostage situation, loss of a staff member in the line of duty, or other potentially troubling institutional event, the institution psychologist can play a crucial role in allowing staff members and/or their families an opportunity to discuss and process their feelings in a manner that prevents them from otherwise leading to intrapersonal and interpersonal difficulties (Linton, 1995). Plans should be coordinated that whenever any problems develop that a mental health professional is available to all employees and family members that need crisis intervention as soon as possible. Major institutional events should always be followed by debriefing group sessions where small groups of staff have an opportunity to discuss their role and feelings in the event that occurred. In many instances, this can be the first realization a staff member will have of the powerful emotions bottled up within them and offer them a forum in which they can see the normality of their reaction. Debriefing groups are most likely to be effective when the members share similar experiences. That is, hostages should be debriefed together, staff members on duty when the incident occurred together and then on to staff members who were not on duty, but still are likely to have significant emotional responses to situations that occurred on their work site. Mixing of the different groups is more likely to lead to greater defensiveness on the part of those most significantly affected. Where possible, debriefing groups for staff spouses and children may also be indicated.

Participation in debriefing sessions has often been made a requirement of effected staff members in the past, but this is not advisable
based on more current research. If a requirement for counseling is
made, it should include an option for individual contact with a psy-
chologist/counselor and the professional providing the contact should
not force an otherwise well-functioning individual to discuss their feel-
ings/thoughts regarding involvement in the traumatic situation. Despite the fanaticism of some regarding debriefings, research has not
been terribly supportive for its having any measurable benefit for participants (McNally, Bryant & Ehlers, 2003). Additionally, it appears to
have a negative impact on at least some of those participating (Advisory Council on First Aid and Safety, 2006).

For those participating, individual follow-up sessions should be
made readily available. The psychologist coordinating the sessions
should not rely on those needing follow-up to come forward voluntarily, either. It is good practice to make notes after each session which
members should be approached again privately to ensure they have
successfully dealt with the situation.

In the correctional field, once a major situation is resolved there is
a tendency to believe that the problem is over. One of the most challenging jobs of the correctional psychologist, then, may be in convincing administration and staff of the necessity of dealing with powerful emotions that are often suppressed out of necessity during the crisis itself. Education of what to expect in the aftermath and an opportunity to discuss one's feelings, cognitions and fears may be crucial to
the continued effective functioning of staff members and the institution as a whole. The only method of making one's job easier in convincing staff of the importance of effective debriefings, when they have
not experienced such traumatic episodes in the past, is education prior
to the event of common reactions and experiences. Finally, though
easily overlooked, the psychologist should ensure an opportunity for
personal debriefing and reflection with the help of an experienced
professional as well. Crisis situations, to be expected in corrections, are
usually short-lived. It is the responses to them that can last a long time.
Probably no one is exposed to a greater amount and degree of the situation, and for a longer period, than is the psychologist. It is easy to
see how one could suffer from significant burnout in the days and
weeks following a significant institutional event when one retains
responsibility for monitoring the inmates mental health, but must also

tend to the needs of staff and their families as well. One should not be shy in requesting assistance, both in managing the acute situation and in obtaining one's own debriefing.

CONCLUSION

The preceding sections offer one a glimpse into the multivaried nature of duties that correctional psychologists have an opportunity to be involved in. In some cases, the duties described may involve a major focus of the psychologists attention, while in others the duties may be part-time or intermittent ancillary responsibilities. In any case, the chances for personal and professional growth in a variety of different capacities are demonstrated. Also clear are the multitude of areas in need of more extensive research investigation that will lead to refinement in their effectiveness in improving outcomes within and beyond our Nation's prison systems. While there are few purely research positions in existence within the correctional field, there is often a multitude of data available for collection or study to the psychologist able to attend to it. The development of relationships with local colleges or universities can sometimes serve as a source of outside employment for the psychologist that can give them access to students and other researchers who can assist in the development of valuable research projects within the institution.

Chapter 4

ESTABLISHING AND MAINTAINING APPROPRIATE RELATIONSHIPS WITH INMATES

WHEN ENTERING WITHIN THE CONFINES of prison walls, one becomes surrounded by men who have spent much of their lives in self-centered attempts to maintain their own happiness. They typically have long histories of using other people for their own selfish purposes and then summarily discharging them from their lives when they are of no further use. Additionally, if at some point it becomes to their advantage to turn on those from whose hands they've fed they are often able to do it without seemingly a tinge of anxiety or guilt. The total lack of sensitivity to others needs and uncaring about the giving side of normal relationships displayed by inmates can be shocking initially and can easily lead to a disillusionment towards the motives of others in general if one loses sight of the special nature of the population you're dealing with when working in corrections and its deviation from much of the rest of society. For this among all else is probably the single largest contributor to the prison population: an extreme selfishness and lack of respect for others; their needs, their rules, their laws.

There is a common misconception that everyone in prison insists that they are innocent. In my experience this has not been true at all. Most of the inmates that I see admit that they engaged in at least some degree of wrongdoing related to their case or outright acknowledge their guilt entirely. What they object to is *how* they were convicted of their crimes. They will sometimes lament at length how the government used unfair methods of catching them in the commission of their crimes, in obtaining evidence or in the use of government informants to seal a conviction in a case where the inmate was never actually caught in possession of illegal contraband. The irony of their complaints that the government plays unfair and doesn't follow the rules in convicting them of illegal acts seems totally lost on them. Rules apparently are made for other people, not for them. Thus, many inmates spend their entire sentences arguing their cases with superfluous appeals that clog the court system trying to somehow manipulate their way out of taking responsibility for their actions. This is the key, they admit wrongdoing, they just don't want to accept the consequences of their acts.

Let's look at one example of the degree of selfishness that is commonly present in inmates. An inmate in his mid-twenties once came to the author in distress, requesting the opportunity to talk to someone about his problems. His chief complaint was that his wife was being unfaithful to him on the outside. The inmate fairly readily admitted that he had, at times, been unfaithful to his mate before his incarceration and that she had knowledge of this. After some time he came to reveal that his wife had actually moved in with a much older and relatively wealthy member of the community in which they were from. In exchange for room and board, she was serving as the gentleman's housemaid while also providing him sexual favors. He also admitted that in his absence she had no obvious way to support herself and his child as she had no previous work experience and little education. She had told the inmate that she was continuing in this role out of necessity.

The inmate, after much discussion, appeared upset at two main things. First, that she was engaging in sexual activity with another man and must be enjoying it or she would not continue to do it. This in spite of the fact, incidentally, that this same inmate had engaged in homosexual prostitution himself in the past out of a sense of financial necessity. Second, that she had not sent him any money. He was rather indignant that given his present predicament that she had been so heartless as to not send him money so that he could purchase snack items from the prison commissary and that this demonstrated her lack of commitment and love towards him. That he was more concerned with getting "twinkie money" than whether and how his wife and child were managing to survive without him clearly demonstrates the incredible egocentricity one routinely encounters.

From this perspective of the prisoner arises a tendency to see others only in terms, then, of their utility. Every new contact leads the inmate to surmise within themselves the value of each new relationship they encounter. If there appears no obvious benefit to be had from someone, the inmate will possess little interest in instigating or developing any type of relationship. Why work for nothing? This leads to some special considerations when large numbers of such inmates are confined within institutions. Certainly they will and do try to take advantage of each other. Inmates will use other inmates or try to gain from their contact with other inmates by gambling to gain money or access to other material goods, or they may provide material goods in exchange for sexual favors. In the absence of money or other material possessions they may try to gain access to those things they desire by forceful intimidation. Singularly, if they are larger and/or stronger than average, in groups if not.

THE NEED TO DEVELOP HEALTHY SKEPTICISM

The prison environment in some ways becomes a place where one can practice the act of conning and manipulating other people. Any success, no matter how small, affords great pleasure to some inmates. Given their access to a very few sources of satisfaction what may appear to the casual observer as a rather insignificant accomplishment can become a substantial source of pride and achievement to the inmate, and even a source of recognition among other inmates. There actually appears to be a drive that has developed within many of these men to overpower other people either physically or psychologically that needs to be satisfied for them to maintain psychological equilibrium. Failure to satisfy this drive seems to lead to feelings of powerlessness, anxiety, depression and other difficulties that often lead the inmate to be involved in the disciplinary process of the prison and/or to come in contact with the *prison psychologist.*

Thus, we may see an inmate who appears to be in a genuine state of suffering. We know that they have antisocial tendencies, but there is no denying their distress. The result? Many of us see this as an opportunity to utilize our skills in providing not only supportive encouragement, but see this as an opening for real, lasting personality reorganization.

After all, one does not try to convince the person who is on top of the world that they are going about things all wrong and begin to rebuild their psychological structures from scratch. Even if they are downright delusional in their satisfaction, they will pay us little attention. No, it is when the *antisocial'*' typical methods of dealing with the world are creating such an inability to satisfy their basic needs that they are at a loss of what to do that we have an opening created whereby we may actually be able to provide a positive intervention within their cognitive framework.

While the foregoing is undoubtedly accurate to a great degree, our need to help others can easily lead us into a trap that only serves to reinforce the antisocial's standard method of dealing with the world. For as soon as we let our guard down and display a desire to assist the inmate in distress, we will often find that they interpret our actions as a sign of weakness. Just as quickly as they became distressed, they may now begin to rework their manipulative tendencies and try to take advantage of us in some manner. It is as if our caring triggers an awareness within them of an opening whereby they may be able to fulfill anew their need to manipulate and thus regain confidence in themselves.

There are numerous difficulties with this turn of events. First, it can easily cause one to develop a sense of callousness towards inmates out of a presumed ulterior motive for any requests for assistance. Second, it can cause one to lose objectivity in assessing the individual inmate and lead one to make later judgments of greater harshness either consciously or subconsciously as a way of obtaining some retribution. Last, and probably most significant, it can cause one to look foolish to other staff members who question how a highly educated psychologist can so easily be fooled by such an obvious liar and manipulator. Of course, correctional staff believe that all inmates are liars and manipulators and thus are not caught making this error very often.

The problem lies when later on you have an inmate with a genuine Axis I psychiatric disorder that truly needs your intervention in getting appropriate treatment and/or dismissal from the typical disciplinary procedures that would be involved if they were not in fact seriously disturbed. If the staff have seen that you have been too easily manipulated in the past, you will have an incredible battle being heard concerning your professional opinions. On the other hand, if they have seen that you have a general distrust of inmates and are not easily convinced of their having genuine mental illness, they will be much more apt to take your advice seriously. Maintaining staff relations will discussed in greater depth in Chapter 6. For the moment the question we will deal with is, given the above facts, how does one most effectively deal with inmates?

PREVALENCE AND TREATMENT OF MENTAL ILLNESS IN CORRECTIONAL ENVIRONMENTS

It is a popular myth among the general population that the incidence of mental disorders amongst prison inmates is exorbitantly high. This idea is reinforced by the greater amount of media coverage of unusual crimes and criminals. The typical offender may never garnish press coverage or only be written up in a minor article in the local paper that is easily missed. Such cases as Charles Manson, Jeffrey Dahmer, Ted Bundy and other similar individuals, however, receive extensive coverage and media play that may continue long after they are apprehended, tried and imprisoned. Local crimes receive scant attention and may actually be intentionally kept quiet to avoid scarring the communities reputation as a safe place to live and work, unless they involve particularly bizarre, violent or unusual circumstances.

The actual figures regarding prevalence of mental illness in prisons are quite variable in the literature, owing to differing operational definitions of mental illness and classification procedures. If one includes the DSM-IV (APA, 1994) diagnosis of Antisocial Personality Disorder (APD) under the rubric of mental illness, for example, the prevalence of mental illness will probably come to at least 80 percent. It is probably better to exclude this diagnosis, however, for two reasons. First, the broad definition described in DSM-IV makes it exceptionally easy to qualify for this diagnosis. In fact, the diagnosis itself appears to be designed as a category to include anyone involved in criminal behavior so that all those guilty of crime can be judged as mentally disordered in some way. This is owed more to societal needs to uphold its cherished values as universal to all "normal" individuals and to deny the inherent greed and self-interest that exists in our biological make-up and is so nurtured by our materialistic society, than to achieve an effective classification system for the mentally disordered. Second, inmates with APD are rarely a concern to mental health professionals.

As a psychologist in a correctional environment you will routinely encounter inmates that meet the criteria for APD to a greater or lesser extent, but in regards to providing treatment and crisis intervention services, you will find these individuals only rarely involved. The exception, of course, is when such treatment involvement is seen by the inmate as a means to an end, such as increased chances for parole, sentence reduction, and so forth. The fact of the matter is, these inmates cause us as psychologists few problems. They rarely decompensate into psychosis and just as rarely present as a threat to harm themselves in any manner. When they are involved in unacceptable types of behavior, the problem is virtually always in regards to their breaking the rules of the institution in a deliberate and intentional manner that will need to be handled by the custodial staff, with mental health personnel having little of value to directly contribute. The fact that we have so little to offer these individuals, are so rarely genuinely asked for help by them and expend so little of our efforts towards them makes them far different from offenders who fall within any of the other DSM-IV categories.

Excluding APD inmates, we can further break down the larger class of inmates diagnosable under the DSM-IV system into three groups. The first, and most significant, are those with major Axis I mental disorders of great severity. There are numerous studies that have examined the prevalence of three primary disorders within this class:schizophrenia, bipolar disorder and major depression. Some of the better studies (Guy et al., 1985; Daniel et al., 1988; Teplin & Swartz, 1989; Hodgins & Cote, 1990; Baskin et al., 1991) have shown prevalence rates for schizophrenia ranging from 1.1 percent to 11.5 percnet, for bipolar disorder from 1.1 percent to 3.3 percent, and for major depression from 1.1 percent to 8.1 percent. The second group of diagnosable inmates are those with separate or concurrent drug and alcohol dependencies. Prevalence rates for drug dependency have been reported as ranging from 11.5 percent to 18.6 percent and for alcohol from 10 percent to 33.1 percent. Finally, the third category of DSMIV inmates are those who would qualify for an Axis II Personality Disorder other than APD. Here we would expect the most common diagnoses to be Narcissistic Personality Disorder and Borderline Personality Disorder, with some incidence of schizotypal, paranoid and schizoid. In female populations, we would further expect an increased rate of Histrionic Personality Disorder. Unfortunately, there are no data currently available that have looked at prevalence rates for these conditions.

From a criminologic point of view, the prevalence of personality disorders other than APD in offender populations is of little concern. These individuals are not considered to be so seriously impaired, generally speaking, to qualify for a plea of insanity or diminished capacity and they do not tend to get involved in physically aggressive acts. Furthermore, by definition, their problems are long-standing and heartily resistant to treatment efforts. From the point of view of the psychologist working within a correctional environment, however, these individuals often present the greatest concern.

First, in the case of borderline and narcissistic inmates, they will often command a great deal more time and attention from both the psychologist and the rest of the correctional staff than the typical inmate. They often will quickly come to be seen as quite a nuisance by most of the staff because they have such a pathological need to receive attention from them. These individuals often exhibit poor relations with other inmates because the narcissists perceive themselves as more similar to the staff (although always considerable better) and borderlines focus their needs for interpersonal acceptance and attention on the authority and power figures in their environment. The staff do not tend to excuse or understand their behavior as emanating from any mental disorder, but instead see them as whiny complainers, troublemakers and manipulators that are purposely trying to interfere with their accomplishing their assigned tasks.

As the psychologist is often the only one that has any degree of understanding of the behavior of narcissistic and borderline inmates, these inmates will often become regular visitors to the Psychology Department. Though they usually do not respond to any treatment efforts, per se, we as psychologists can sometimes offer advice for methods of dealing with their immediate complaints that can serve to minimize the degree of problems and frustrations encountered by all concerned. Sometimes our advice is even followed. Surprisingly, though in prison, these inmates are usually not interested in any form of self-evaluation or treatment, but have acquired the APD's preference for blaming the "system" for all of their travails. Almost inevitably, the psychologists perceptions of these inmates, while perhaps a more informed one, results in much the same dreaded feeling of other correctional workers when we are thrust into an interaction with them.

Their inevitable failure in personal and interpersonal pursuits within the correctional environment, which also characterized their life before incarceration, will often lead them to periods of significant decompensation and despair. In fact, these inmates are most likely to require crisis interventions and most likely to be involved in suicidal gestures and attempts. The time requirement involved in their cases is, consequently, often quite considerable and, unfortunately, often ineffective in producing any measurable long-term improvement in their functioning.

As far as the seriously disordered Axis I offender is concerned, they will often occupy less time and attention to the institution psychologist than the non-APD Axis II inmates. It is not unusual to see schizophrenic, and sometimes bipolar inmates, who appear barely stable upon entering the institutional environment become increasingly stable and well-adjusted over the first several weeks of their commitment. For these individuals, the correctional environment is actually more predictable and structured than life on the street, and thus works to minimize episodes of major disorganization that may be caused by the stresses of independent living. These are inmates that in previous generations would have likely spent their lives in mental hospitals, but today are forced to attempt to adjust to life as the rest of us do or be punished for their failures. It is probably wise to keep a handy list of some sort of inmates with Axis I disorders whether or not they successfully adjust to the institutional environment or not. Due to the chronic nature of their problems, they may decompensate under conditions where their normal routine is interrupted or under periods of intensified stress. As a result, in the event of a major disturbance within the institution which necessitates a lockdown in which inmates are refrained from leaving their cells for a period of time, it wise to pay particular attention to these inmates' ability to adjust to the situation and to ensure that those prescribed medications continue to be medicated as usual. Along the same lines, when such an inmate gets involved in a violation of the institutional rules and is placed in disciplinary segregation, it is wise to closely monitor their functioning on a regular basis. In some cases, you may need to intervene in ensuring their continued successful functioning by quietly arranging for a more lenient sentence for their rule infraction (if appropriate) or by other means designed with the particular inmates needs in mind. For example, in some cases you may wish to ensure that the inmate is given a cellmate to help avoid the possible deleterious effects of social isolation. In other cases, you may need to ensure they are not given a cellmate because their paranoid nature will not allow them to feel comfortable enough to get adequate rest with a "stranger" in the room. Obviously, knowledge of the particular inmate based on previous contacts and experience, as well as ongoing interactions with the inmate should lead you to be able to decide the conditions most conducive to their continued positive functioning, while not impeding the correctional requirements of the institution in which you work.

A sometimes troubling and delicate situation can occur when dealing with an inmate who has strong elements of both a thought disorder and APD. These inmates often have a penchant for getting into trouble and though they indeed have symptoms of serious thought disorders, there is little doubt that they possess the requisite presence of mind to understand that the actions they engage in are wrong and they should, therefore, be held responsible. The complicating matter is that in the course of the disciplinary process (e.g., being handcuffed, escorted to segregation, etc.) their thought disorder may often cause them to make poor behavioral choices that make their situation more difficult and alienate them from staff. The major complicating factor in these cases is that other correctional staff members will see only the manipulativeness and verbal/physical aggressiveness of these inmates, without being able to take into account their other difficulties. Once labeled a troublemaker, always a troublemaker, and it is hard for other staff to consider the influence of significant mental illness in a person they clearly see as manipulative because the standard perception is that the mentally ill are too "crazy" to be manipulative. Though this type of inmate should not be immune to correctional procedures, care may need to be taken in their apprehension and punishment phases to avoid unnecessary cognitive decompensation of the inmate and unnecessary complications for all. Once again, good communication with staff members can ensure these cases are handled properly.

ANTISOCIAL PERSONALITY DISORDER VERSUS PSYCHOPATHY

Partially in response to the limitations of the diagnosis of antisocial personality disorder, there has remained an element who have argued for an adjunct or entirely separate entity of sociopathic or psycho-pathic personality disorder. This essentially involves an individual that not only meets the criteria for APD, but appears to exemplify it in all its glory. While many inmates in any correctional institution can easi-ly qualify for the APD diagnosis, a much smaller group would fall within the psychopathic realm. If considered within the APD diagno-sis, then, we can view psychopathy as a dimensional trait with milder levels more associated with perhaps the typical inmate and more se-vere levels encompassing the "psychopathic personality." It is proba-bly wise and increasingly likely that future updates of the Diagnostic and Statistical Manual will subdivide the APD diagnosis into at least two separate entities. Hare (1980) has devised an objective assessment method based on structured interviews and file reviews for assessing psychopathy. The Psychopathy Checklist (PCL-R) rates the subject on 20 different dimensions (Hare, 1986, 1991) that measure the primary characteristics of psychopathy with a total score that can range from 0 to 40. Subsequent research has shown that the instrument has predic-tive validity in estimating recidivism rates of criminals for both violent and non-violent crime. For example, Hart, Kropp and Hare (1988) examined 231 penitentiary inmates released under supervision and followed for an average period of 40 months. Results showed that recidivism rates were 30 percent for the lowest scorers (24 or less), 62 percent for the intermediate group (25-33) and 90 percent for the psy-chopathic group (33-40). Harris, Rice and Cormier (1991) looked at violent recidivism of 169 inmates released into the community over a 10-year period. Amongst offenders with an initial psychopathy score less than 25, 21 percent recidivated violently while a full 77 of the psy-chopathic inmates did.

Research on recidivism, treatment selection and treatment outcome are increasingly using the PCL-R as a useful tool in predicting and assessing outcome. When the topic of designing effective correctional interventions was discussed in Chapter 1, it was noted that the most powerful and efficient interventions should focus on the highest risk offenders. It would appear that the PCL-R is one of the most reliable methods of identifying such offenders so that they may be targeted for specific interventions. The psychologist working in the correctional field will no doubt be increasingly exposed to the PCL-R and famil-iarity with it is recommended. In fact, the American Psychiatric Asso-ciation has considered using the PCL-R as an adjunct to the diagnosis of Personality Disorder, Antisocial Type (Hare, Forth & Strachan, 1992). If this were to occur it would definitely increase the reliability and specificity of this diagnosis and make familiarity with the PCL-R a requirement for correctional psychologists.

MANAGING THE MENTALLY ILL INMATE

Perhaps fortunately for us as psychologists, our role in the correctional environment in relation to the majority of inmates is not so much to effect lasting personality change as it is to assist in treating psychological complaints and/or behaviors which are disruptive to the overall functioning of the institution. We are not asked to cure the narcissist, but merely to minimize his disruptive influence. We are not asked to abolish the suspiciousness of the paranoid schizophrenic, but to minimize the likelihood of his delusions resulting in aggressive acts against staff or inmates. Although many of the mentally ill in correctional settings also possess characteristics of APD, rather than target their criminal attitudes that may have led to them violating the law in the past or may influence them doing so in the future, our role is typically to assist them in managing their primary mental disorder in the present. This is not to belittle the psychologist's role in the institution, for the problems these offenders present to correctional staff are unique and often misunderstood. Without the services of a mental health professional on site, it is easy to see how the treatment of the truly mentally ill could fall into the realm of the less than humane, which ultimately would work to the benefit of no one.

Consider the case of an inmate previously diagnosed with bipolar disorder who became noncompliant with lithium soon after entering the institution. He showed mild cognitive abnormalities which made him appear distracted, likely the result of auditory hallucinations. The inmate was distrusting of <u>staff</u> and refused to acknowledge psychological symptomology. He claimed that he did not need his medication and did not like the side effects they caused him (a familiar refrain to be sure). Although in some institutions forced medication may be an option, typically in such situations it becomes necessary to monitor these inmates gradual decompensation until they reach the point of qualifying for commitment to a psychiatric hospital. In this inmate's case, his mild cognitive disorientation led him to get into frequent difficulties with being in unauthorized places. On one occasion he was found to be taking a shower when all inmates were required to be in their cells for a daily count of inmates to occur. On several other occasions he was found to be missing from his work detail to be found wandering on the recreation yard or gazing off into the sky. Over time he became increasingly resistant to talking to psychology staff and also seemed to possess increasingly less presence of mind and self-control to avoid being in a place other than where he was required to be. During this period of time, the inmate was placed in disciplinary segregation on several occasions.

On his first placement, he had the presence of mind to try and argue that his mental illness had caused him confusion, such that he should not be held responsible for his actions. Since he was refusing treatment (lithium) against our advice, I informed him that he would be held responsible for all of his actions in full unless and until he was actually being treated for mental illness. The inmate received no sympathy from the correctional staff who felt him to be manipulating and faking. Approximately two weeks after being released from segregation, he was returned there for being somewhere other than where he was required to be again. The staff on his unit demanded a statement that he was competent and showed a great deal of annoyance with his case. They appeared as incredulous in this case as in his first offense at suggestions that he did, indeed, suffer from a mental illness. Perhaps to reinforce this point and in an attempt to get the inmate to cooperate in his treatment, his psychologist released him from responsibility for his actions on mental health grounds with an understanding between the psychologist and the inmate that he would comply with his medication regimen.

Upon his release, the inmate continued to be non-compliant with treatment. He was successful in remaining in general population for several weeks, although this was largely due to staff's overlooking several transgressions of the rules. Finally, he was again locked up. On this occasion he displayed surprisingly less interest in having the psychology staff release him of responsibility and seemed to be less concerned with being in solitary confinement. There had been an increasing withdrawal and decompensation by this time, yet he remained adequately oriented to his surroundings and certainly presented no danger to himself or others. Although it began to become clearer that we would eventually need to intervene in his case, the waiting game continued. It is an unfortunate complication of court decision-making that we have to wait for such individuals to decompensate to virtually infantile levels of behavior before we can intervene against their will.

After the fourth time he was placed in segregation, the attitude of the staff began to change. They too, became aware of increasing oddities of his behavior and finally seemed willing to acknowledge that his behavior was not a total result of manipulativeness and antisocial tendencies. Interestingly, only as the inmate reached his lowest levels of functioning did the staff begin to reach out and try to make concessions for him in an attempt to help him successfully cope with the institutional environment. I am not trying to belittle the staff because they truly did everything they could think of once they were able to clearly see the inmate was genuinely ill. Unfortunately, it was too late.

The staff, without our departments intervention, dropped disciplinary action and returned the inmate to general population. Because he seemed to get "lost" so easily, they placed him in a different housing unit and job assignment, such that the distance he would have to travel to get from his cell to the dining hall and to his job were minimized. They felt confident that the short distances would ensure his success, despite my advice that the inmate was becoming too disconnected from the outer world for these procedures to be effective. In fact, it was my preference at that point to maintain him in segregation for disciplinary reasons so that I could most effectively monitor his behavior and where his personal safety could most effectively be ensured until he decompensated to the point of allowing his transfer to a psychiatric hospital. The irony of my arguing for him to be locked up instead of helped was not lost on me at the time, but since the inmate presented no immediate threat to himself or others, I did not stand in the way of the custodial staffs' plan. The inmate became increasingly unresponsive and withdrawn, entering an almost catatonic state at times within the next couple of days during which Psychology and Medical Services were summoned on a couple of occasions.

We were then called again when the inmate was observed to be wandering around on the recreation yard with his pants pulled down. In the course of responding to the referral, the recreation yard supervisor approached the inmate, requested he pull up his pants and was responded to by the inmate with an attempt to assault him. The inmate had to be handcuffed and carried by four staff members for a distance before half agreeing to proceed on foot. When evaluated by our department and medical personnel the inmate was uncooperative, and speech was largely limited to requests to remove his handcuffs. He appeared very distracted by auditory hallucinations and may have, by his appearance, been suffering from visual hallucinations as well. He carried an unkempt appearance and an odor from not washing in several days. In short, the inmate appeared as a textbook example of a schizophrenic in the midst of a psychotic break. He was escorted to a holding cell until he could be transferred to a psychiatric hospital for forced treatment with antipsychotic medication.

The example is provided not only as an example of cases that involve the institution psychologist for management, but also to demonstrate the difficulties that interject into inmate care at times from the staff's general tendency to dismiss mental health factors as irrelevant and/or factitious until an inmate is virtually totally incapacitated. It is hard to blame the staff for the simple reason that the base rate for faking mental illness from their standpoint is so high that they are well-served in the assumption that everyone is faking. However, it can occasionally be quite frustrating feeling as though you have to convince each staff member one by one that your professional opinion is more accurate in a given case than their intuitive judgments. I will save a further discussion of this issue for the chapter on staff relations.

INMATE MANIPULATIVENESS

A psychologist is often seen as possessing a great deal of power and influence within the system by inmates. They also may be seen as empathic and willing to listen. As a result, inmates with desires that they have been unable to have fulfilled by other staff members within the institution will often approach a psychologist, particularly a new psychologist, for assistance. Their hope is that you will empathize with them to a sufficient degree to accept their cause and take it upon yourself to ensure that they receive a justified result. In the vast majority of cases, the psychologist will not be the appropriate individual for them to make their request to. Likewise, in the vast majority of cases the inmate realizes this and is merely exhausting all avenues before conceding defeat. However, because of your perceived power and prestige, they may feel you could change the course of events in their favor were you won over to their cause. As an individual psychologist we will have various levels of influence within an institution, and in regards to particular staff and situations. Typically, one's influence over ordinary custodial management decisions is quite limited, particularly for the new psychologist. One reason for this is there tends to be clear and direct written policies for handling most situations that must be adhered to. Secondly, convincing a staff member to make an exception from usual procedure is not likely to be forthcoming for a new psychologist who tends to be greeted with great initial skepticism by other staff members.

Although one may easily become intoxicated with an inmate's claims of your superior prestige and power owing to your special position within the institution, I have found it better to severely downplay to the point of exaggeration how much influence I possess with other departments and in regards to custodial management decisions. I have similarly found it wise never to accept responsibility for solving an inmate's problems, regardless of how justifiable their desires may appear. Although I am willing to empathize with an inmate's personal dilemma, I am also more than willing to refer them back to the appropriate staff member for an appeal of the issue in question, share in their feelings of helplessness and attempt to explore with them some strategies for coping should matters remain in the undesired direction. I am also willing to assist inmates in trying to understand the other perspective of the situation and to help them in knowing who the best person to talk to about their problem is and how to go about presenting their difficulty in such a manner that optimizes the possibility of a successful outcome. Don't misunderstand, I do not believe in trying to make an inmate more successful at manipulation. However, many inmates have a very poor frustration tolerance and when they do not get their way immediately can become their own worst enemy in pursuing the correction of sometimes legitimate problems. As a result, the situation they are in may present an opportunity to perform some counseling on maintaining their cool, focusing on the most significant issues and presenting their requests politely and appropriately. Of course, I always stress that this won't necessarily lead to a successful outcome, but will likely maximize their chances.

There are times, of course, where we as psychologists may indeed have some influence over the situation in question. It has been my preference to deny such powers even then, although there are times in which one might follow-up the situation with other staff in an effort to assist the inmate to obtain a better outcome. In such cases, one's efforts are best left unbeknownst to the inmate himself. In this way, one can greatly reduce the number of trivial complaints that inmates will approach you with for no other reason than to try to manipulate the system to achieve their personal ends. Make no mistake about it, inmates communicate with each other. If an inmate finds you helpful in overcoming the initial decisions or desires of other staff members, he will quickly share that information with other inmates and the number of referral requests you will receive will mount exponentially. This is not a good use of the psychologist's services and can significantly distract the psychologist from fulfilling the legitimate responsibilities they have. Additionally, you will not endear yourself to other staff members if they observe you to be questioning their judgment and checking up on them on a frequent basis. In those rare situations that I do follow-up on an inmate's problem, I prefer to go directly to the staff member responsible, inform them that inmate X has come to speak with me and ask them to explain what the situation is. This usually results in exasperated exhalations and rolling eyes, but they are usually quite willing to explain their perspective without defensiveness. More often than not they will also let you know how the inmate has misrepresented his case to you or what policy restriction governs the decision that was made. In either case, you can easily dispatch the outcome as justifiable within the system as a means of resolving any lingering feelings of guilt you might possess over taking no action whatsoever.

It should also be mentioned that inmates in some systems, particularly those heavily laden with bureaucratic methods of resolving issues, will sometimes try to threaten and manipulate staff members through administrative complaints or outright lawsuits. If you work in the correctional system long enough, especially in a field such as psychology or medicine, you should anticipate having lawsuits filed against you. I have observed that some staff members become quite nervous about this, particularly when it is a first-time experience, but there is usually little to be concerned about. If you are following generally accepted practices and your own institutional policies in providing services, any lawsuits should be summarily dismissed without prejudice. In fact, I have always taken the tactic of encouraging inmates to file grievances against me if they feel justified in doing so because it is a relatively healthy and innocuous way of discharging their frustration and anger. The only problem it creates is in its creation of further paperwork for the institution and the courts, but at this point there are systems set up in both places to handle these inevitable actions. It is best to let such complaints run their course than to further inflame inmate passions or allow them to manipulate you by trying to prevent such behavior. Moreover, it is my recurrent experience that if one genuinely shows no concern about threats of such actions, inmates usually won't find the experience pleasurable enough to carry through with the effort involved.

SERVING DIVERSE POPULATIONS

As mentioned above, inmates communicate extensively with each other about their contacts with staff members, including the psychologist. Additionally, you will find that they similarly keep tabs on each other and are very curious about virtually all activities that occur within the institution. It is important, then, that you not only perform your job with professionalism, but that your professionalism is obvious to others in some way. An example of this is in regards to the client population that you serve.

It is important to ensure that you have a degree of sensitivity to all of the different cultural groups represented among the inmates of the institution. It is natural for all of us to subconsciously approach that with which we are familiar and somewhat stay away from those things that seem strange or mysterious to us. Practically speaking, within an institution this tendency can manifest itself in two primary ways to cause unnecessary difficulties. First, inmates from the same cultural group as yourself will tend to feel more comfortable talking with you and seeking you out for services. Inmates from different groups will have greater difficulty trusting you and approaching you. I suspect this is a more powerful component of behavior among inmates than even exists in the general population. As many of those we see in prison grew up in socioeconomically disadvantaged and more culturally segregated environments, their view of other cultures may be quite limited and/or negative. Second, when working within the institution you might subconsciously shy away from groups of inmates of a different cultural group as your own and have more of a tendency to approach those of a similar nature. Over time, these two tendencies can cause you to basically lose touch with all but the inmates most similar to yourself. It is not usually a conscious choice or even preference, but can easily occur. As it becomes more evident, inmates from other cultural groups will become even more distrusting and reluctant to approach you and you might even be cast by the inmates as being prejudiced, becoming a target of anger or violence.

To prevent this from happening it is important to be honest with yourself and review your activities from time to time. When you see the aforementioned group of inmates of a different cultural persuasion, become aware of the feelings of anxiety, overcome them and approach them. They will likely feel as uncomfortable as you, but I guarantee you will earn their respect for your action. With repeated efforts you will approach them more naturally and they will become more accepting of your presence. Another consideration is to evaluate the inmates that you see on a regular basis. If you find your caseload to be severely skewed towards a single cultural group, you would probably do well to cultivate therapy cases from other groups. After all, if you are not careful, you will find that the inmates are aware of the situation before you are. Realize that this may entail being more persistent with some inmates in encouraging their therapy involvement than you might ordinarily be because you will need to overcome their natural tendency to shy away from you.

Sensitivity to these issues also requires that you make an effort, perhaps, to become more aware of different cultural practices and behaviors. For example, it has been my experience as a white male that this group is the one that most readily approaches me. Additionally, when they approach, they tend to be quite straightforward telling me that they desire assistance and in describing what their problem entails. On the other hand, it has been my experience that Hispanic inmates in general population will not usually come forward with their problems. However, if they are privately asked about how they are doing, they will often readily reveal to me the problems they are having. Finally, my experience with black inmates has been that they are also much more reluctant to request help and are the most guarded in individual sessions. Unlike Hispanic inmates, black inmates are more likely to approach me when they are in need of assistance, but they often vaguely describe their problems in a joking manner which makes it hard to discern if they are serious or just playing games. Although it may have taken me a while to pick up on this, I now make it a point to go ahead and make an appointment for a private interview with black inmates that jokingly talk about needing to see me. More often than not, they have issues to discuss, but the cultural environment they grew up in makes it particularly difficult to openly ask someone for assistance. This is especially true when the person being asked emanates from a different ethnic group.

RELATING TO PHYSICALLY THREATENING INMATES

Occasionally when interacting with an individual inmate in the normal routine of things you will get one who will make veiled threats against you in the course of conversation and engage you in a generally intimidating manner. Frankly speaking, if you are working in a correctional setting, you must expect such behavior from time to time. The truly surprising fact may be how little it actually occurs. When it does, however, I think it is important to recognize that you are likely dealing with someone who is merely interacting with you in perhaps the only manner he knows how. The inmate has learned that he can obtain some degree of respect or acceptance from peers in this manner and can ward off authority figures whom he has a great deal of negative feelings or anxiety towards. The anxiety of interacting with someone of greater power than they can be relieved through the reaction formation of actually acting as if they were the more powerful individuals in the relationship. In the absence of significant evidence of an Axis I disorder, it is probably best in the majority of cases to simply ignore the behavior and ensure that one does not let it influence one's own behavior, reactions or functions.

If you are screening an individual who responds in this way, proceed through all your typical inquiries without omitting items just because you see little chance of obtaining an appropriate response. Additionally, totally inappropriate responses or refusals to offer any responses on the part of the inmate can be calmly reframed by the therapist as emanating from the inmate's understandable difficulties trusting the therapist along with reassurance that the interview is for the primary benefit of the inmate. Statements along this line will usually result in inmates responding to you in some way. The mere act of them talking is typically sufficient to calm and relax them, thus increasing their cooperativeness in the interview as whole. It is probably a good idea to emphasize your availability in the future to inmates should they desire someone to talk to or have any questions. You will have communicated to the inmates your willingness to help them should they need it and that you are not going to be intimidated by their behavior. If you succeeded in calming them down and opening up to any degree at all, you have begun to train them on more effective communication techniques which will hopefully be built upon during the time of their incarceration.

A belligerent inmate who shows evidence of a thought disorder will obviously need to be handled in a more delicate manner. The most effective technique is often to withdraw from the usual course of the interview altogether and try to make a connection with them before proceeding. This may involve asking them how they came to be incarcerated, about their family or whatever they may be willing to talk about. In this process you can assess their ability to control their emotions, the extent of their cognitive disturbance and uncover the nature of any delusional ideas they may possess. This will allow you to decide if they are capable of proceeding through the interview or if other actions need to be taken. In a standard institution (not designated as a medical treatment center) you will not encounter such situations often. More common is the paranoid schizophrenic that may be wary of you initially, but can become fairly easily allied with by discussing how they arrived at the institution. A willingness to listen in these cases and to offer empathic responses will usually assist in separating you from any negative delusional processes they may have developed in regards to law enforcement personnel.

Whenever one is dealing with threatening or intimidating inmates it is important to remember that one works within a large institution full of potentially violent offenders. It is also an institution full of coworkers committed to keeping it a safe and orderly place to do business. Whenever one feels truly threatened, consideration first and foremost needs to be on personal and institutional safety. It is harder for psychologists to call for assistance in dealing with belligerent inmates, I think, because many of us are reluctant to admit that we cannot handle an interpersonal interaction independently. We think because we are psychologists that we are uniquely qualified to be able to settle down an aggressive inmate or that we are somehow invulnerable to an inmate assault because the inmates will all see that we are there to help and serve them, thus never even considering making us a victim of aggression. This is where one must truly examine the extent of our own pride and egocentrism.

It is not a failure to call for assistance when an inmate looks to be on the verge of aggression or to ask a co-worker to sit in on the interview to provide an increased measure of safety. It also will not cause you to lose the respect of your co-workers. Quite to the contrary, you are far more likely to enhance your reputation with co-workers who will appreciate your calling on them for assistance and who will also get a chance to see just what goes on in the mysterious environs of the psychologist's office. It has been my experience that the perceptions of laypersons to my interventions with inmates are usually quite positive even in instances where I may have personally judged my actions to be ineffective and clumsy. The quickest way to lose respect of co-workers and make yourself a victim of aggression, on the other hand, is to think one uniquely qualified to singularly handle even the most difficult of situations and inmates. Even when you may get through the situation with success, by acting alone you have taken on unnecessary risk, caused yourself unnecessary stress and anxiety, and placed not only yourself, but others at risk should the situation not have gone as well.

As far as the inmate's perceptions of interviewing them in the presence of other mental health professionals or non-professionals rather than on an individual basis, their response is often indicative of the level of danger that truly exists. An inmate who is genuinely upset, particularly one with mental illness, will usually show little concern about another individual being present and be able to fully engage themselves in the interview. A more psychopathic inmate with greater control of their actions, however, will tend to point out the presence of the other staff member and seem to derive some pleasure from the fact that you are sufficiently intimidated by them to be too "afraid" to see them alone. The latter type of inmate is least likely to benefit or even require your intervention, while the former will still be able to get the assistance they need. In regards to confidentiality, the security of the institution and its staff always override such concerns. For more information on this issue, refer to Chapter 2.

BUILDING TRUSTING AND APPROPRIATE RELATIONSHIPS

It is standard procedure in the institution in which I practice to individually interview each and every inmate upon their entrance into the institution. This allows one to get a firsthand look at every inmate, as well as opportunities to converse with them and do a summary review of their case. Obviously, the first priority in these interviews is to identify new inmates with significant mental illness. Typically a quick interview will reveal any signs of major mental illness that may currently be active, as well as residual symptoms of more dormant conditions. It can also allow you to identify those inmates having particular difficulties adjusting to the conditions of confinement or the adjudication proceedings of their case. For example, a 20-year-old inmate who has never served more than a few days at a time in the local jailhouse may come to you only a few days after receiving a sentence of 20 years or more. The shock may still be quite active and a careful assessment of their level of desperation and depression is certainly in order. By offering a few minutes for them to talk about their feelings, encouraging them to proceed with their lives one day and one step at a time, and sometimes, encouraging them to have hope that their sentences may be reduced on appeal, you may be able to circumvent a process in which they spiral into depressiveness and suicide. It also tends to reduce their sense of isolation in knowing that someone seems to understand and care about their problems and will be there for them to talk to. Actually, the surprising fact is that most inmates in this type of situation are remarkably resilient and, while no doubt being quite afraid inside, are quite able to hold things together without professional assistance.

Even in the absence of serious mental illness or significant adjustment difficulties, the intake interview can allow you to identify inmates that have profound Axis II syndromes that will almost assuredly bring them into repeated contact with you in the future. Finally, some inmates will quickly reveal their strong antisocial tendencies with deep resentment of authority figures in such a way as to virtually guarantee that they will be disciplinary problems for the institution in the future.

Most inmates that you interview upon their entrance into the institution will fall into none of the aforementioned categories. Most will be reasonably well adjusted (at least in regards to the population in question), stable and experiencing no significant problems that they cannot cope with independently. In fact, this interview is in many cases your only contact with the inmate at all. It is quite important, then, to give each of them your full attention and establish good rapport. If you succeed in making them feel comfortable with you and trusting in your genuine desire to assist them in any manner necessary, then they will be much more likely to seek you out in the future should they develop problems. This is important, because if they don't seek you out later when problems develop, it is likely that they will internalize their emotions until they are no longer able to control them, creating problems not only for themselves, but others. It is my belief that this can sometimes be the single most effective tool the psychologist has for influencing the institution environment by heading off both current and future problems before they erupt into broader institutional management concerns.

It is easy once the initial intake interviews are completed to sit back and wait for others to either come to you asking for assistance or wait for staff members to call about inmates they have some concerns about. Certainly this will be a successful strategy much of the time and when you are shorthanded or particularly busy, this may be all you can hope to accomplish. When this does not take up your entire schedule, however, you should strongly consider making "rounds" throughout the institution. Although this may seem like wasted time to some, it can be time well spent. First of all, it gives you a chance to see different parts of the institution and make yourself more aware of what is going on outside your department. Additionally, it gives you exposure to inmates in varying environments. Thus, for example, you can watch how your chronic schizophrenic inmate is functioning in their typical environment or perhaps see the inmate who this morning complained of dire depression in your office laughing with his or her friends. In short, it gives you a more complete picture of those inmates you follow on a regular basis. Additionally, it gives other inmates a chance to approach you with questions, concerns and problems.

I have been amazed at how these wandering visits can produce impromptu sessions or elicit requests for emergency assistance from inmates who state that they have been considering contacting the department for a while. Apparently, the ease with which they can approach you during these times is able to tip the balance towards seeking help. Even in the absence of seeking out regular inmates for observation or "drumming up business on the fly" being out on the compound often elicits approaches from inmates I would normally have no contact with who come up to tell jokes, talk about happenings within the institution or the world, or even talk about sports. Again, some would see this as time wasted, but I believe it serves a very important public relations role. Inmates, those who approach and those who watch others approach, begin to see you as open and trustworthy. You are perceived not as the highly educated doctor who deals only with "crazies" and "psychos" in your mysterious lair separated from all others, but as an approachable, caring individual who has respect and concern for the inmate population. Inmates will also be quite cognizant of those who approach and interact with you for any reason. In fact, high status inmates are often the ones who will feel comfortable enough to engage in light conversation with you. This may encourage other inmates to look up to them, but it also encourages other inmates to feel comfortable approaching you. All of these contacts normalize the act of talking to the psychologist, so that those who speak with you are not automatically assumed to have serious psychological problems.

A statement should probably be made, as well, regarding our role in maintaining institutional security. I believe if we are successful in being perceived as trustworthy and genuinely concerned about inmate welfare we can undoubtedly intervene at the earlier stages of crisis situations with inmates before their emotions and tensions build to the point of their getting into verbal or physical altercations with staff or other inmates. Additionally, given that prisons are occasionally the site of disturbances greater than at the individual level, with these disturbances being extremely costly in both physical damages to the institution and physical and psychological injury to staff members, building good rapport with a diverse range of inmates can also make you a likely individual to be given advance information about a pending disturbance from an inmate who needs a staff member they can trust to give the information to.

MAINTAINING PROFESSIONAL DISTANCE

Although one should strive to maintain positive relationships with the inmate population whenever possible, it is also important to recognize that inmates are not and should not become your "friends." There is sometimes a fine line between being friendly and being friends, however, and if some general rules are followed the line should be easier to maintain. Inmates should be referred to by their last names only, such as Ms. or Mr. Jones. Using their first name breeds too much familiarity and breaks down the formal professional demeanor that should be maintained. Using a nickname that the inmate may go by is even more harmful and also reinforces their criminal lifestyle by using street names associated with their criminal associations. One should always be polite and respectful in manner and tone, unless unusual circumstances require a harsher approach. Not only should you endeavor to maintain these practices, but you should demand that inmates follow them with you in return.

It is unwise to reveal personal information about yourself, your family or your private life with the possible exception of hobbies or spectator sports you may be interested or involved in. Oftentimes inmates have relatives and friends residing in the surrounding community and if they have too much information about you the walls between your personal and professional existences may begin to break down. With the necessity of having to be on guard and impersonal at work, it is important for one's psychological health to be able to feel relaxed and comfortable being open and genuine in your private life. Never have secrets between you and inmates or agree to maintain secrets that inmates share with you. You are never the inmates ally against staff or institution procedures, you are merely a professional resource that they can choose to use if they so please.

The idea of maintaining professional distance from inmates is actually easier than many might think. Most inmates are rather distrusting of others and are often quite tight-lipped even to each other about their criminologic and personal histories. As they are used to maintaining interpersonal distance with each other, they are not offended or surprised when their relations with staff are kept that way as well. The only exceptions to this are the naive inmate who has not yet "learned the ropes" and still responds to others like he did on the outside, the inmate who is intentionally trying to obtain information about you for mischievous sport, and the non-APD Axis II inmate who always deviates from expected behavior patterns.

The fairly simple procedures to be followed to maintain appropriate professional distance are very obvious and simple to those with any experience in the correctional field. They are offered here more for the novice or those considering entering the field both for one's own protection and for a better understanding of how correctional psychology may be seen as different from other subfields. In fact, in most areas of psychology we would probably try to engage and encourage quite opposite tendencies in ourselves and our clients as a way of deepening our relationships so as to provide maximal psychoemotional support and healing.

An additional method of maintaining professional boundaries between yourself and inmates that may be available, depending on the institution you work in, is to work in correctional posts within the institution. I have had the opportunity during my career to work in correctional officer positions in which I was in charge of the daily affairs of an entire housing unit as the frontline officer or in charge of supervising the compound and coordinating inmate movements within the institution, among others. The value of working these positions are considerable. From the standpoint of the present discussion, it allows inmates to see without a doubt that you are a cooperating member of the correctional staff. You may be there to assist them when it is necessary and possible for you to do so, but you are always a member of the correctional staff first. There is no question what side you are on. One may argue from a psychological perspective that this is also healthy for inmates to see someone they may have a positive impression of as being helpful and concerned for their welfare in a position of authority, thereby helping to alter some of the negative associations they may have built up towards authority figures in their life.

Chapter 5

DEALING WITH MALINGERING AND DECEPTION: THE INTERVIEW

LIFE FOR THE CORRECTIONAL PSYCHOLOGIST would be simplified if one could ascertain whether someone were mentally ill merely by asking them and then treating the symptomatic complaints. The reality of the situation is that many truly mentally ill deny their conditions on inquiry and many of those who claim to suffer the symptoms of major mental disorder are actually normal (here defined as the absence of an Axis I condition). While this may provide for the necessity of having mental health experts on staff and our long-term job security, the amount of time and energy one must spend just trying to sort out fact from fallacy can be frustrating at times. One cannot work effectively as a psychologist in the correctional field without maintaining a degree of skepticism regarding the verbal reports of inmates and a good working knowledge of how to detect malingering and recognize signs of mental disease in those making no such complaints.

Training in graduate school and through clinical experience usually prepares us to adequately detect mental illness during the course of a clinical interview. In regards to inmates, one should make an effort to check on any documentation regarding history that may be available on an inmate and never discard any record of prior mental health treatment. However, it is not unusual for inmates entering the correctional environment to have a relative paucity of background information available for review, especially in regards to medical and psychiatric histories. In the absence of any red flags in their files, a brief standard interview is normally sufficient to uncover active or residual symptoms of major mental illness. If any doubts arise, additional interviews, testing or background checks should be conducted to avoid seriously mentally ill or unstable inmates from not being detected.

The detection of malingering significant symptoms of mental illness is not an area that is often covered adequately, if at all, in graduate school. Experience is often effective in honing one's skills, but early failures to detect malingerers can sometimes be embarrassing and professionally painful. Additionally, some clinicians remain quite reluctant to accuse individuals claiming mental distress of faking their symptoms. Obviously, this is tantamount to calling someone a liar and our societal upbringing teaches us that this is not only impolite, but potentially dangerous. If one is to survive in a correctional environment, however, and maintain the respect of the inmates as well as the staff as competent in the field of psychology, reservations about identifying malingerers must be quickly overcome.

As noted in the chapter on inmate relations, it has been my finding that the majority of inmates will admit to being involved in some of the illegal activities for which they are incarcerated, but object to taking responsibility for these behaviors and accepting of the resultant consequences. Do not underestimate the time and energy that an inmate will expend in an effort to avoid responsibility for their behaviors. If they believe that their best hope of eluding punishment for a crime committed on the outside or a disciplinary infraction they are charged with within the institution is to fake mental illness as a defense, they will do this to the best of their abilities. Additionally, there are inmates that will feign symptoms of mental disease in an effort to procure psychoactive medications for their own recreational use or for sale to other inmates. For some inmates any medication that affects their mental functioning may be seen as desirable to obtain. Some may wish to have antipsychotic medications for the heavy sedation it imposes, others may seek Prozac or Lithium in an attempt to obtain a minor stimulant effect. Even medications not thought of as having high potentials for abuse are occasionally misused for recreational purposes.

Feigned complaints of mental illness are fairly common in a correctional setting. If one works in a facility that performs a significant number of forensic evaluations to determine inmates' competency to stand trial or criminal responsibility for their crime, much of your time will be devoted to accurately classifying true cases of mental illness from those attempting to escape responsibility for illegal actions they have engaged in. Even in the fulfillment of general duties as an institutional psychologist, though, the issue is one that will frequently occur. Most often a good clinical interview can lead one to make an accurate assessment of the genuineness of the inmates' symptomatic complaints. In the present chapter, techniques for distinguishing true cases of mental illness from malingering by means of effective interviewing is discussed. More formal testing can be reserved for cases in which one is having more difficulties making a confident decision or in cases that have a higher likelihood of ending up in court and thus may necessitate a higher level of proof of one's clinical judgment. In Chapter 6, then, a review of the most commonly used assessment devices in the correctional field is offered with empirical data on each measures' effectiveness in detecting malingerers.

ASSESSING MALINGERING IN THE CLINICAL INTERVIEW

The positive news concerning the role of detecting malingering in inmates is that the vast majority of them are not very good at it. We can assume a fair degree of antisocial tendencies in anyone that engages in such deception regardless of what their ultimate goal may be, and the large majority of such cases clearly fit the diagnosis of Antisocial Personality Disorder (APD). APD's have several shortcomings in their character that makes their efforts to feign mental illness easier to detect than the average person. First, these are impulsive people. Their decision to attempt to feign mental illness is also frequently a decision made on impulse. As a result, it is unusual for the APD to have taken the time to research what mental illness they will try to fake and what the major symptoms of that mental illness are. The result is that they present only a small portion of the symptoms of a major mental disorder and show no indication that typically related problems are present. They also do not show the usual progression of difficulties commonly seen. Thus, someone claiming intense anxiety is noted to sleep quite restfully or an individual claiming intense depression appears to interact quite easily and happily with peers.

A second aspect of the APD that often prevents them from effectively feigning mental illness, related to the first, is their typical lack of significant education. Many of these individuals have not completed high school, much less college, and have never received any formal education regarding the principles of abnormal psychology. So, once again, their understanding and knowledge of mental illness tends to be quite naive. This results in an incomplete presentation of symptoms, an overplaying of symptoms, an unusual progression of the claimed illness or claims of possessing highly unlikely symptoms (e.g., multiple personality disorder or bizarre psychotic symptoms).

The third aspect of the APD that makes them relatively easy to decipher is that they typically have a long history of well-documented criminal behavior. At each instance in which they came into contact with the "system" information was obtained from them and about them. As a result, by the time they reach adulthood there is usually quite a paper trail behind them. Initial claims of significant mental illness in someone with an extensive history of antisocial behavior and absolutely no history of mental difficulties is unlikely in most cases. Even when one develops an initial psychotic disturbance associated with schizophrenia during the early twenties one would normally expect to find a significant prodromal phase preceding actual psychotic symptomatology.

APD's tend to have a barren emotional existence with little corresponding understanding of the affective realm of human behavior. Thus, their reports of distress and depression are typically devoid of any outward behavioral manifestations of such problems. For them to say they are depressed is to be depressed and further proof is unnecessary. There is also a narcissistic component that enters into the equation here. They will often see themselves as sufficiently streetwise to outsmart a psychologist, who may be seen as not too intelligent as evidenced by their concern for other's problems. Even when the APD knows what symptoms they are supposed to have, they may have too much self-pride to lower themselves to actually display any of the symptoms they verbally report. This can be particularly true when in the company of other inmates, as the APD may be reluctant to lower their status in their peer group by becoming known as mentally disordered. Further manifestations of this narcissistic conviction of being able to manipulate the psychologist are a tendency in some to brag to their peers about how they are successful conning you in conversations which can be overheard by other staff or may even be communicated directly to other staff members in some cases, and a strong tendency to make no attempt to display or report symptoms of mental illness when the psychologist is not present to appreciate their actions.

If faced with a clear-cut situation of malingering, it is best to challenge the subject immediately with your clear conviction that they are malingering. In many cases they will quickly relent and, in my experience, perhaps even ask you what tipped you off. Sharing your insight into how you detected their charade is unwise, even in the most pathetic attempts. I have discovered in reviewing inmates files on more than one occasion that an inmate suspected of malingering had, indeed, made such attempts in the past and been detected. Some inmates will seem to feel obligated to try anew whenever a new psychologist happens along. It is probably best not to assist in their efforts to refine their technique.

In situations where there is strong suspicion of malingering, but one is unable to feel absolutely certain, you may wish to imply your belief that they are malingering without blatantly accusing them of such. Usually without sufficient attention from the psychologist their tenuous belief in their ability to foil you will fold and they will seek other avenues of manipulating the system. Not becoming overly involved in initial, suspect, cases of mental illness can prevent a great deal of unnecessary time and work involved if the inmate becomes emboldened by perceptions of early success. Early challenges, direct or indirect, are an often effective means of preventing this problem.

Finally, APD's do not report symptoms of mental illness without a desire to achieve some end. Those with true mental illness often come to the attention of the psychologist because they are acting strangely or because they request assistance. APD's symptoms arise suddenly in response to a need. Usually, their need is to escape prosecution for an act of criminal conduct. In contrast, a person with true mental illness who has been involved in a serious violation of law or rules will not only tend to show clear signs of mental disease, but is also more likely to be coy about sharing their symptoms of mental illness and to show remorse and acceptance of responsibility for their actions.

In summary, APD inmates may use claims of mental illness to escape responsibility for their actions or in an effort to obtain psychoactive medications. Their attempts are usually naive and relatively easily discerned with a careful review of the patients history and a good quality clinical interview. In cases where the distinction between true illness and malingering is less clear, feedback from the direct observation of the inmate, particularly by non-mental health professionals, is often helpful in cases where the inmate might present symptoms only in the presence of the psychologist.

Rogers (1997) has published the authoritative manual on the detection of malingering and deception. Some additional indications of malingering that can be assessed in the course of the clinical interview that is described in that text are offered in Table 5.1.

USE OF PSYCHOLOGICAL TESTS TO ESTABLISH OR CONFIRM MALINGERING

In many cases where one is asked to perform a psychological evaluation to determine the presence or absence of significant mental illness for forensic purposes, the first issue that comes to mind is the necessity of administering standardized psychological instruments as if they were both effective and authoritative methods of accurately separating these two distinct categories of testees. The reality of the situation is that they have the potential to both help you and hurt you in these situations, and sometimes may only serve to unnecessarily complicate the situation. One's best method of detecting malingering remains in the clinical interview where your training and experience in dealing with genuine mental illness should guide you well. One can be virtually assured of always having greater knowledge of a mental disorder and greater firsthand experience with it than an individual trying to malinger its symptoms. Additionally, it can often be much more challenging to maintain symptoms of mental disease over a prolonged period of time than a malingerer initially imagines.

Having the opportunity to covertly observe an inmate's behavior at different times during the day and/or interview staff members who spend time with the inmate in your absence can often reveal the substantial difference in behavioral presentation that a malingerer will present when an evaluating mental health professional is not present. In the correctional environment these measures are usually readily available as the inmate's cell may be under video monitoring or supervision of correctional staff. Additionally, monitoring of inmate correspondence and phone calls is often performed in a correctional setting for security reasons, but can also present hard-core evidence in the

TABLE 5.1
CLINICAL SIGNS OF MALINGERING EVIDENT DURING A
CLINICAL INTERVIEW (ROGERS, 1997).

1. Malingerers tend to overact. They may believe that the more bizarre they act, the more psychotic they will appear.
2. Malingerers are often quick to call attention to their illness whereas true schizophrenics are reluctant to discuss their symptoms.
3. Malingerers do not display loosening of associations and other related cognitive signs of schizophrenic illness.
4. Claimed symptom picture in malingerers often does not correspond with any standard diagnostic entity.
5. Malingerers often claim a sudden onset of delusions/hallucinations, whereas in real cases onset is usually gradual over a period of weeks.
6. Malingerers are more likely to make contradictory claims regarding their symptoms. When challenged they may sulk or laugh.
7. Malingerers may accuse interviewer of thinking they are faking, whereas true psychotics rarely do.
8. Malingerers are more likely to repeat questions about their "illness," to answer slowly or pause before responding. Also more likely to give "don't know" answers.
9. Malingerers do not typically show signs of residual symptoms such as impaired relatedness, blunted affect or peculiar thinking.
10. Real hallucinations are associated with congruent delusions in the vast majority of cases. (88%)
11. Schizophrenic hallucinations tend to be intermittent rather than continuous. Malingerers may claim that their voices never cease for long periods of time.
12. In cases of true auditory hallucinations, both male and female voices are heard 75% of the time. In only 7% of cases is the message vague and undecipherable. Malingerers are more likely to have difficulty describing voices and content of message.
13. Schizophrenic patients usually have developed superstitious behaviors to make voices go away or to reduce influence through distraction such as engaging in certain activities, changing posture, listening to radio, etc. Malingerers typically will claim that "nothing helps."

form of the inmate's own voice or writing, admitting to their deceptive activities. If one is brought into court with the objective of having to convince a jury of an inmate's normality in the face of continued malingering, showing video or audiotape of the inmate, letters he has written or hearing testimony of how he acted perfectly normal in the psychologists absence from correctional officers is typically quite convincing and clear-cut. Introducing psychological tests whose ability to detect malingering can be subject to question in some cases and a source of diverting attention from the more concrete evidence described above will only make your job more difficult, particularly if the test does not seem to support your conclusions.

In the following section, we review a case in which use of psychological testing instruments were not utilized due to the availability of significant data from effective interviews and observations that were wholly sufficient in answering the referral question. Following this, an additional case is presented in which input was requested regarding the potential parole of an inmate. The example displays how clinical interviews accompanied by good documentation can sometimes preclude the need for psychological testing in order for appropriate recommendations to be made.

Case #1

Subject is a single male in his mid-twenties referred for an evaluation of his competency to stand trial. Subject was arrested for being a felon in possession of a firearm. He was living with his mother at the time of the arrest. Subject claimed on interview to have suicidal thoughts, hallucinations which include command voices, insomnia and memory impairment. He appeared confused and to have great difficulty understanding explanations of the purpose of the evaluation being conducted. Subject did not answer when asked what sentence length he was facing if he were to be found guilty, but showed basic understanding of the prosecutor, judge and defense attorney's role in the courtroom. During the course of evaluation the subject often repeated questions back to the examiner in an apparent query as to their meaning. He showed lability of mood that did not respond to medication and showed poor eye contact. The only times when he made spontaneous detailed remarks occurred when he talked about his bizarre symptoms. Subject talked about seeing a small green man named Brian who gave him commands to hurt himself and others. Subject added that when he doesn't comply with these commands that the little man makes things (such as rodents) come after him in his dreams.

Records reveal that the subject was referred for a psychological evaluation in the fourth grade due to significant academic difficulties and what was described as being easily frustrated and having difficulty remaining seated. The evaluation resulted in a tested IQ of 71 and placement in a special education setting. On interview, his mother claimed that he remained so designated until he dropped out of school in the seventh grade (at age 14). Mother also reports that subject never got along with his siblings, that he had mental problems and desperately needed help. She indicated that he had been on disability for years and had been treated by a psychiatrist. She also confirmed his complaints of having insomnia, visual and auditory hallucinations and added that he needed to be told things "over and over."

Documented treatment history began with a request for a psychological evaluation from a juvenile court judge at the age of 15. Several days after this order was made, the subject was seen in an outpatient clinic on an emergency basis. The psychiatrist who saw him noted that the subject represented a risk to others, particularly those in a position of authority. Subject was further described as a powder keg and to be suffering from increasing elements of the "psychotic components" of his illness. Another mental health worker at the time noted inappropriate laughter and agitation. Subject's mother refused at the time to comply with recommendations for hospitalization, but agreed to provide subject with prescribed antipsychotic medications. No further corroborating evidence was able to be located documenting subjects claims of mental illness.

Juvenile justice records revealed that the subject had actually been suspended from school in the seventh grade following an assault on his junior high school coach. During his sixteenth year subject was arrested on six reported occasions for felonious level offenses. These included armed robbery of a motor vehicle and for shooting another person on two different occasions. His adult criminal record is too extensive to outline in detail, but includes at least three felonious assaults, three attempted murder charges related to firearms and a murder charge. Of interest in his case was that his brother was a codefendant in several of his cases and he had another accomplice in other cases. His records reveal no further mental health treatment beyond that listed above. It should also be noted that further investigation into his background revealed that the medication prescribed at age 15 outlined above in his mother's report was discontinued by the doctor when the subject continued to report that he was taking it regularly long after the prescription supply should have been exhausted.

In responding to inquiries during the course of the evaluation the subject often responded "I don't know" to even basic questions that most severely disturbed individuals can answer.

When confronted about his behavior, he would sometimes become mute and other times use profanity in his angry responses. He described no delusions, illogical or tangential thinking. He claimed to be unable to provide his age, current whereabouts or home address. During his stay he placed numerous long distance telephone calls to various family members without assistance. Subject initially reported thoughts of suicide upon entering the evaluating facility, at which time he agreed to a no-harm contract whereafter he denied any further thoughts of self-harm.

Inmate has four children by four different mothers, providing no financial assistance to any. Interviews with subject's probation officer revealed that he was not receiving disability payments but had held various short-term jobs through a temporary placement service and has been able to hold a job when forced to by the threat of possible negative consequences. Claims of insomnia were in contrast to correctional officers observational reports that he slept approximately 90 percent of the time.

During taped phone conversations he made to family members, he indicated that he was not going to reveal any information about himself, and that when he got out he would have to make sure that he killed anyone who gave him difficulties because he would get a significant prison sentence whether he killed or merely injured them anyway. He was also heard to warn his mother about being careful on the phone since the calls were monitored and to coach her on what information to give others. He clearly indicated that he was making an intentional effort to reveal no information to the examiner in his case.

No formal testing was conducted due to the extensiveness of the subject's evasiveness and lack of cooperation during interviews. Additionally, information gathered suggested it was superfluous. More than sufficient information was gathered through a detailed investigation into his history, a thorough clinical interview and detailed observations of his behavior. In short, the subject clearly had a long history of antisocial personality disorder with a long history of aggressive acts, irresponsible behavior and lack of respect for societal rules and authorities. He had no prior legitimate record of thought or affective disorder. His use of accomplices in his crimes, ability to establish sexual relationships and his many telephone calls made to family members during the evaluation argues against the social withdrawal normally seen in a psychotic illness of the nature he claimed to possess.

The subject also showed a strong desire to talk about the psychotic elements of his illness which contrasts with the typical authentic case. He frequently responded to inquiries with "I don't know" responses, feigned perplexity or responded only after considerable delaying tactics. In short, the only evidence of the existence of mental illness was his self-report and reports from his mother, both of which were highly unreliable and frequently in direct contrast to documented facts.

Case #2

Subject is a male in his upper twenties upon which information was requested by a parole board regarding his suitability for release prior to fulfillment of his complete sentence and/or suggestions on conditions of probation. At the time of the request the inmate had been incarcerated at the present institution for approximately 10 months on charges of attempting to defraud senior citizens in a telephone fraud scam. During this period of time he had had five documented contacts with the psychology department. On the initial interview upon arriving at the institution the inmate was noted to exhibit a superficial charm and cooperative attitude, but to also appear to be carefully and selectively offering information about himself. A review of his record indicated that he offered no information about himself that was not explicitly and directly requested and that what information he did freely offer corresponded very closely to what was described in his presentencing investigative report. In fact, the inmate had given no information to the interviewer that could not have been obtained from his file report. He significantly underplayed in the interview the extensiveness of his criminal record and made no mention of sexually-oriented infractions or problems. He denied any history of mental illness, but freely reported that he had regularly used cocaine and methamphetamine since the age of 17. He expressed strong interest in obtaining placement in an intensive drug treatment program. This, incidentally, contrasted with his file documents which indicated that he had not used any drugs in the 12 months prior to his arrest. It should be noted that at the time, successful completion of the intensive drug treatment program qualifeed some offenders for a sentence reduction of 12 months as an inducement to participate.

Inmate had no contact with the psychology department until approximately nine months later. It was at this time that he was nearly far enough along in his sentence to qualify for entrance into the intensive drug treatment program. During the interview for this program the inmate started out with a respectful and cooperative demeanor. He was informed of his ineligibility for time-off consideration because of specific exclusions based on his prior record and also questioned as to the veracity of his claims of drug problems. He quickly became very angry, uncooperative and threatened to take legal action to en-sure his entrance into the program and time off for such participation. The examining psychologist noted strong antisocial personality traits demonstrated by his use of subtle and blatant manipulation, and alternate use of hostility and humbleness in attempts to influence the examiner. Noting the presence of a long history of sexual offenses, some of which resulted in charges still pending, the interviewing psychologist suggested a referral for treatment in a sexual offender program.

On interview two weeks later, being interviewed by a different psychologist, the inmate requested an evaluation for the sex offenders program. At the beginning of the interview, subject repeatedly invoked his newfound commitment to Christianity and a genuine desire to straighten out his life. He was unnaturally humble and pious in presentation. He avoided discussion of his sexual offenses, but after persistent questioning began to respond more directly to inquiry. Inmate talked of engaging in voyeuristic behavior during his early adolescent years. Later, he began driving around and masturbating while parked and observing females in the community. He progressed to also calling attention to himself during these forays and engaging in exhibitionistic acts. Finally, just prior to the arrest for which he was incarcerated, he appeared to engage in a greater degree of following his victims around. In an incident just prior to his arrest he followed a victim from her residence, forced her off the road and then attempted to enter her vehicle while masturbating. During the interview, the inmate admitted to all charges for which he was convicted that were documented in his file. He displayed numerous inconsistencies in his reports during the interview and made statements unlikely to be true given the nature of his offenses. He initially claimed to be under the influence of drugs when engaging in such behavior and to have no memory of these events.

Later, he described the events in question and admitted that his involvement in such acts preceded his use of drugs. He also stated at one point that he would satisfy his sexual urges to masturbate while watching females in a matter of minutes when sober, but when under the influence would drive around for days at a time compulsively engaging in these deviant acts. He denied being able to achieve orgasm during these acts, being excited by his victims reactions to exhibitionistic acts nor having masturbatory fantasies of a deviant nature, thereby denying any source of sexual motivation for continuing to engage in such acts. He denied all responsibility in the final case regarding following the victim, assaulting her vehicle or masturbating before her (these charges were still pending).

At the beginning of the interview, the inmate denied ever using drugs other than occasional experimentation. He did report some use of alcohol which initially was reported as a mild problem secondary to his sexual difficulties. When he was told that there was no provision for granting reductions in sentencing for participants in the sexual offenders program, his story made a dramatic shift. He then downplayed his sexual urges and deviancies and claimed that his primary problem was alcohol. He stated a belief that he could control himself when not inebriated and that effective intervention for his alcohol problems would control all of his difficulties. He made repeated attempts to move away from an interest in the sexual offenders group with repeated references to his newfound religious faith that, coupled with sobriety would keep him on the "right path." Not surprisingly, the exact point of his religious conversion was quite pliable and inconsistent as well, with earlier reports that his most recent offense was indirectly authorized by God as evidenced by the great success he experienced. Additional review of his case led to the same finding of his earlier encounter: that he would not be eligible for time-off consideration for participation in the drug program. Upon reaching this point in the interview, his calm, humble and pious demeanor was shaken, making him appear hostile, threatening, and ready to explode. He insisted that he had reviewed the relevant law and found no statements that would exclude his participation in the program and of receiving the benefit of a year off. He further insisted on being placed in the program and that he would fight any attempts to exclude him from the year off with legal interventions. As with the sexual offender program, then, his interest appeared to lie with personal benefit regarding his sentence with no actual interest in receiving treatment.

The treatment history, as reported by the subject, appears to have been minimal engagement in individual therapy and AA meetings when these were made mandatory of him by various judicial bodies.

The subject reports a brief marriage which ended after a violent argument whose cause the subject was unwilling to divulge. He downplayed the level of violence during this episode and denied previous altercations, though he stated that his wife entered a shelter for abused women upon leaving him.

Available records of juvenile adjudications reveal that subject was charged at least once for indecent exposure and once for voyeurism. He had numerous traffic violations and apparently had his license suspended for driving under the influence of alcohol. He subsequently obtained half a dozen citations for driving under a suspended license. He had been charged with contempt of court more than once, as well as several charges for resisting arrest and eluding police. He had two previous convictions for telemarketing fraud and two lewd conduct convictions. He had several prior convictions for possession of cocaine and methamphetamine and had threatened witnesses in several of his cases with violence if they provided adverse testimony.

On the basis of the foregoing information, I believed there was sufficient information to respond to the request for information in the absence of testing. In fact, it is hard to imagine what purpose would be served by submitting the subject to psychological testing, as one could probably do a more than adequate job of predicting the results. The case clearly involves an individual with strong antisocial personality traits. Additionally, he has the added appeal of possessing sexual deviancies which have shown a long and clear progression towards increasing levels of direct contact with the victim and an increasing propensity for violence. Both his antisocial attitudes and sexual problems are likely exacerbated by drug and alcohol use. The subject takes no responsibility for his actions, has no empathy for his victims and possesses a significantly high risk of engaging in further criminal actions in the future. Additionally, the progression of his sexual offenses is a particular concern and he would appear to represent a threat of being a sexual predator in the future. In an individual with this level of aggression, it is not an exaggeration to wonder if he might not progress toward the raping and/or murdering of a future victim in an attempt to satisfy his deviant sexual/aggressive needs while trying to simultaneously prevent additional incarceration. He would not seem to be a good candidate for parole and any probation should be carried out under maximum conditions of supervision.

The cases above highlight the ability to make good clinical judgments and conclusions based on good factual evidence and quality clinical interviews. The use of psychological tests should be reserved for in-stances where these sources of information are incomplete or otherwise lacking. Thus, the use of psychological tests is not necessarily re-quired to detect instances of significant deception or outright malingering. The importance of keeping good clinical notes on therapeutic contacts and screening interviews is also demonstrated in the second case by an opportunity to construct an informed decision based on the professional observations and input of several different staff members carried out over a prolonged period of time. In those cases where prior information is not available or is insufficient, there are several tests that can be useful in obtaining important and relevant information that is easily defensible in court. It is to these instruments that we turn to in Chapter 6.

Chapter 6

DEALING WITH MALINGERING
AND DECEPTION:
PSYCHOMETRIC EVALUATION

CHAPTER 5 DISCUSSED THE USE of clinical interviews and observation to detect inmates attempting to malinger a significant mental illness. In the present chapter several of the most commonly used psychometric devices for assessing suspected cases of malingering are reviewed and discussed. This is not meant to be a comprehensive overview of the various testing products that are used for this purpose. Instead, those instruments with the longest histories, most common use and most extensive empirical validation for this purpose are examined.

Only psychometric instruments which possess some validity scales in regards to cooperativeness and honesty of the subject should be used in forensic settings. Additionally, tests whose measures are too obviously sampled should be avoided. Thus, it is recommended that an instrument such as the Beck Depression Inventory (BDI) be avoided. Although useful in some settings, the BDI has no method of detecting malingerers and its content is not only obvious, but also dramatic. As a result, it could make one's life more difficult than necessary to face an opposing counsel on the witness stand arguing that an individual is faking and suffers from no significant mental illness, when the attorney presents your own test items showing that their client is reporting significant suicidality, weight/appetite disturbance, feelings of depression, and so forth.

You should be prepared to defend the value of any test you use as well as the results in a manner that is understandable to the average juror. If you cannot explain your findings and where they came from in a clear and concise fashion, then any testimony you render can be effectively obfuscated by an efficient attorney. If an attorney can cause you to engage in long diatribes on the technical aspects of a test to the point where everyone in the courtroom is sufficiently confused, then any actual results reported will be significantly discounted if not lost altogether. Several common psychological tests will be examined for their usefulness in meeting the appropriate criteria for forensic evaluations when psychological assessment instruments are necessitated. Specific research pertaining to each instruments ability to detect malingering is also discussed.

THE RORSCHACH INKBLOTS

Reluctance to Use the Rorschach in Forensic Settings

The use of the Rorschach Inkblots (Rorschach, 1921) in a forensic evaluation has an advantage of presenting the examinee with an unstructured situation that makes the production of disingenuous responses more difficult. It would appear to take a degree of sophistication that many correctional examinees are not capable of to respond to the stimuli in a manner that suggests significant mental disturbance while simultaneously not looking so disturbed as to make a mockery of the process altogether. Someone with knowledge of schizophrenia, for example, may be able to put forth a good effort on a self-report questionnaire with limited answer choices, but be at a loss as to how to transform their knowledge of the disorder they are feigning into a believable compendium of Rorschach responses.

It is unfortunate that the anxiety which may rush through a malingering inmate confronted with the Rorschach Cards is sometimes exceeded only by the anxiety of the examiner in utilizing what some still regard as a less valid and reliable assessment instrument than the "objective" tests routinely given. It is not uncommon for the psychologist examiner to break out in a cold sweat in response to visions of being placed on a witness stand against a young hostile attorney attempting to defend one's ability to extract significant personality data from a bunch of inkblots. Such concerns are more a symptom of the examiners misinformation and lack of appropriate knowledge concerning the use of the Rorschach than there are realistic concerns about the agreeableness of the courts to accepting such testimony. This unsupported fear probably emanates from one's exposure in the academic arena to psychologist-educators that are particularly uninformed and thus hostile to the Rorschach. It is an interesting fact that the Rorschach enjoys wide respect by practitioners and researchers worldwide, though respect from traditional academic environs remains elusive (Watkins, 1994; Weiner, 1997).

It is in the legal arena of practitioners, lawyers and judges, of course, where one's concern about the acceptability and validity of the Rorschach is most significant. In this regard, the Rorschach has been noted to be the second most popular personality assessment instrument used in forensic cases (after the MMPI) and is quite well regarded and respected in the courtroom. Meloy, Hansen and Weiner (1997) conducted a computer-based search of Rorschach legal citations between 1945 and 1995 which resulted in 247 identified cases. Of these, only 26 cases (10.5%) were identified in which the reliability or validity of the Rorschach findings were made an issue. Furthermore, when Rorschach data was limited or excluded in these cases, it was usually due to inappropriate use of the test data by the "expert" witness rather than a shortcoming of the test itself. Other findings are even more encouraging. Weiner, Exner, and Sciara (1996) looked at 7,934 cases in which psychologists presented Rorschach testimony and found only six incidents (.08%) when the test was seriously challenged. In only one instance (.01%) was the testimony based on the Rorschach declared inadmissable as evidence.

Concerns about the ability to defend Rorschach data in court usually originate in mistaken impressions regarding the empirically validated degree of reliability and validity which the Rorschach method possesses. This, too, is unwarranted. There is substantial and convincing evidence available attesting to both the reliability and validity of the Rorschach method (Atkinson, 1986; Parker, Hanson, & Hunsley, 1988; Weiner, 1996; Weiner, 1997) when used in accordance with the principles outlined by Exner (1993). In fact, reviews have found reliability and validity estimates to be essentially comparable to those of the MMPI. Additionally, the Rorschach is further strengthened by the impressive degree and quality of its published normative data using a variety of subject populations (Exner, 1993; Gacono & Meloy, 1994).

The most notable negative review in regards to the psychometric properties of the Rorschach is that done by Ziskin and Faust (2009). Their review, however, was not done impartially and comprehensively as a means of getting at the true value of the Rorschach method. Instead, their intended purpose was to collect only negative data in an attempt to provide interested attorneys with ammunition to use in an attempt to discredit any unwanted testimony. As pointed out by Weiner (1996), references to their work by opposing attorneys can be effectively parried with a reference to the author's own preface which clearly indicates their intentional avoidance of any scientific and research data that may be seen as supportive of the expertise of mental health professionals and/or the tools they use.

The Rorschach Inkblots have a high degree of recognition as a psychological test among the lay public. They also have a great deal of mysteriousness attached to them in that most people are rather incredulous, or even disbelieving, that one can surmise anything about personality dynamics from what an individual sees in a set of inkblots. This can actually be a strength of the test during testimony in that it is assumed to be a commonly used and accepted test (everyone has heard of it) and most laypeople have their interest piqued when discussion of how it works is initiated. If handled effectively, this increased interest can be used to educate jurors in how the test actually works in a clear manner that will cause your testimony to be accepted and receive good attention. It is unfortunate, though, that some psychologists will confuse and lose their audience through lack of effective preparation. Additionally, some psychologists seem to have a need for their own ego gratification in glorifying the mystical aspects of a poorly understood test in order to maintain the mysteriousness and intellectual superiority of their special position.

Effective testimony should be simple and straightforward and one should be prepared to explain how each score relates to its empirically derived interpretation. Projective hypotheses should be avoided, as should any attempts to interpret single responses or cards. When asked about what a particular response means by an attorney, the answer should be a simple, "nothing." Only the collection of responses taken together, scored and compared against the results of others can lead to empirically validated interpretive statements. The test can be presented as not a window into the subconscious, but as a means of determining how one "sees the world and solves problems." All jurors are able to accept that each of us has our own unique ways of organizing and viewing the world and that the test gives us a picture of how an examinee performs such tasks in relation to others. Simple examples cannot only demystify the test, but prevent confusion and boredom from overcoming your ultimate diagnostic inferences. Thus, it has been suggested (Weiner, 1997) that you may offer an explanation such as the one below in explaining W, D and Dd codes to the jury as one example of the types of information that the test gives and how it is derived:

> For example, some people when reporting what they see tend to use the whole blot while others have a tendency to focus on minute details in responding to the cards. Those who focus on the whole blot and ignore the detail are like people in life that don't pay much attention to detail and may miss many things going on around them because they focus only on the big picture. Those who see only the details and don't tend to organize the whole blot are more like those we say can't see the forest through the trees. That is, they get so caught up in details that they may miss the big picture.

In providing explanations such as this, we serve the dual role of providing expert testimony in an effective manner and demystify the role and functions of the psychology field. What may begin as a test that seems impossible to defend or explain to the layperson becomes one no more difficult than any other. Additionally, your willingness to explain the test in an easily comprehended manner should result in your testimony actually garnering greater respect amongst the jurors.

Research on Detecting Malingering With the Rorschach

Numerous researchers have examined whether significant alteration of scores can be achieved by those attempting to respond to Rorschach stimuli in a manner designed to fake psychosis. Although methodological shortcomings within individual studies predominate, there is substantial consistency of results across situations and methods. Early studies found fairly consistent differences in protocols of those suspected of malingering including frequent card rejections, expressions of confusion, repeated questions about test directions and an attitude of pained compliance (Benton, 1945; Feldman & Grayley, 1954; Rosenberg & Feldberg, 1944; Wachspress et al., 1953).

Netter and Viglione (1994) compared the Rorschach protocols of 20 schizophrenic subjects to 40 non-patient, non-schizophrenic, subjects randomly assigned to either a control or malingering condition. Approximately one-third of malingering subjects were able to successfully fake the disorder. Score alterations produced by subjects faking abnormality in such analogue studies include reduced number of responses, slow reactions times, frequent inanimate and animal movement responses, vague or poor form responses, and responses with bizarre, aggressive, sexual anatomy, blood, fire or explosions in their content (Bash & Alpert, 1980; Easton & Feigenbaum, 1967; Feldman & Grayley, 1954; Rosenberg & Feldberg, 1944; Seamons et al., 1981).

An example of how analog analyses, used in many of the research studies to date, can be misleading was provided by Schretlen (1988) in a review of malingering studies on the Rorschach. He noted inconsistent findings across studies in regards to the number of Popular responses reported by malingerers. Schretlen pointed out that the studies reporting an increase in Populars used subjects actually suspected of malingering, while the studies reporting a decrease in Populars used subjects instructed to fake abnormality for artificial reasons.

Bash and Alpert (1980) constructed a "malingering score" composed of 13 Rorschach characteristics empirically found to be related to malingered protocols (each scored either 0 or 1). While the reported results did not break down results on each of the 13 characteristics, comparison revealed that suspected malingerers obtained significantly higher scores than did three other groups suffering from actual psychiatric conditions.

Ganellen et al. (1996) found the only differentiation between a group of malingerers and true responders among a sample of forensic study cases was that the malingerers produced significantly greater numbers of responses with dramatic contents (blood, fire, explosions, sex, aggression and morbids). The lack of homogeneity in the "true" sample and the method of identifying malingerers, however, makes the study difficult to draw firm conclusions.

Several recent studies have utilized the tactic of including as a comparison group, subjects who have been specifically trained in aspects of psychotic illness and then asked to respond to the Rorschach as if they were suffering from such illness. This may most closely approximate the conditions present in the more sophisticated malingerer with personal knowledge or education regarding the signs and symptoms of the disorder they are pretending to have.

Albert, Fox and Kahn (1980) solicited six Rorschach protocols from each of four different groups: psychotic inpatients, uneducated malingerers, malingerers educated about psychotic illness and normals given standard instructions. The resulting protocols were submitted to Fellows of the Society for Personality Assessment with instructions to develop a diagnosis and assess them for possible malingering. Results showed that uninformed malingerers were diagnosed psychotic as often as were actual psychotics. Additionally, educated malingerers were actually diagnosed as psychotic at a higher rate than actual psychotics. Although the study involved the "blind" interpretation of unscored Rorschach protocols and was not able to be replicated for methodological reasons (Schretlen, 1988), the results are nonetheless disturbing in the apparent low ability of experienced professionals to distinguish true psychotics from those malingering such symptoms in some cases.

Mittman (1983) used a similar procedure in which 90 clinicians with experience in Rorschach interpretation diagnosed a packet of five protocols. The experimental groups included inpatient depressives, inpatient schizophrenics, uneducated malingerers (asked to fake schizophrenia), informed malingerers (also asked to fake schizophrenia) and normals given standard instructions. Results showed that uneducated malingerers were diagnosed as schizophrenic significantly less often than were actual schizophrenics. However, judges were not effective at distinguishing between the informed malingerers and the true schizophrenics.

The Rorschach workshops (1987) Alumni Newsletter (cited in Perry & Kinder, 1990) reported positive preliminary results from their long-term study of malingering on the Rorschach. In their report they noted that 5 of 15 non-schizophrenic psychiatric inpatients with contact with true schizophrenics were able to produce a Rorschach protocol in which they achieved a SCZI value of 4. However, none were able to produce a SCZI of 5. This suggests that using a cutoff of 5 should be reasonably effective at avoiding misclassifying malingerers while still correctly classifying the large majority of true schizophrenics. This confirms other evidence for the value of the SCZI in such cases (Exner, 1991). Weiner (1997) indicated that many APD's naturally obtain a score of 4 on the SCZI, but rarely realize a score higher than that.

Research to date has not consistently supported the use of the Rorschach, taken singly, in reliably discriminating between the protocols of malingerers and schizophrenics. Current knowledge suggests that the finding most commonly occurring in the literature when subjects are asked to malinger symptoms of psychosis was a reduction in overall responses (Perry & Kinder, 1990). Taken together, the results suggest that educated malingerers are able to reproduce protocols that are difficult to differentiate from those of true psychotics, however, they are incapable of producing a large number of responses that are consistent with their desired portrayals of the results. Additionally, they may give a significantly higher number of dramatic responses (those involving fire, blood, sex, explosions, morbids, and aggression), as they may "overplay their pathology" to a degree that makes their efforts transparent. A careful attention to the examinees performance and reactions to the test should be carefully documented as a means of supporting any later accusations of malingering which may be contested legally. The examinee who claims an inability to concentrate may be noted to maintain clear prolonged focus to the task. The examinee who will not give a scorable protocol on the MMPI or WAIS-IV due to an insufficient ability to maintain a period of lucidity may display a calculated approach to the Rorschach, or the examinee whose WAIS-IV performance implies imbecility may give away their intelligence with the sophistication of their responses on the Rorschach.

What the studies reviewed herein seem to consistently lack is experimental subjects with something to lose. That is, subjects in many of the reviewed studies participated with no real consequence of being detected and, thus, no strong motivation to succeed. The emotional turmoil that one would encounter if successfully malingering results on the test meant the possible difference between life and death or imprisonment versus freedom would presumably be considerable. Just as likely, this type of affective discomfort would make one less, rather than more, likely to be able to effectively maintain a convincing picture of significant psychopathology for extended periods of time. Additionally, research subjects instructed to fake pathology in many of the studies reviewed above possess a higher degree of intelligence, education and sophistication than is commonly encountered in a correctional setting. Finally, an important aspect not assessed in research studies on attempts to malinger significant psychopathology that is to some extent extraneous to the test is the behavioral presentation of the examinee.

A malingerer too actively engaged in "beating" the test may give himself away by not engaging in consistent verbal and physical response styles. There is also an intimidation factor, I believe, with the Rorschach in malingerers which other tests lack. Even with some preparation or prior knowledge of the syndrome they are attempting to portray, it is unlikely that most malingerers will have a clear conception of how to transform this knowledge into corresponding performance on the Rorschach. As a result, mere introduction of the test can itself cause a prospective malingerer to lose confidence in his ability to maintain the charade, particularly if already fatigued by several days of interviews and tests. It is not unusual for such individuals to lose heart and begin to return to their typical method of functioning or, at least, play their role with less consistency and enthusiasm. Finally, when used as one technique among many in an assessment battery, the ability of the malingerer to maintain consistent performance and behavior across all tests and situations should become a task too great to maintain without significant error. As a result, in practice, we would expect those attempting to malinger to be somewhat less successful than those included in the literature reviewed herein with the Rorschach an important component to the process of uncovering disingenuous claims of mental illness.

Use of the Rorschach With Correctional Subjects

Gacono and Meloy (1994) have published a compendium of information on the Rorschach protocols of subjects with antisocial personality disorder. The high incidence of APD's in samples of malingerers and correctional populations generally make the data an important benchmark for comparison. Some of the major differences between APD's and normal subjects are summarized below.

Affect

APD's are more affectively avoidant than are non-patient males with a reduced affective ratio and an average production of only half as many color responses as the normal male sample. Color responses that are given show impaired emotional control with Pure C responses more common and a FC:CF+C ratio averaging 1:3. Not surprisingly, the presence of space responses is substantially higher in APD's.

Interpersonal Relations

APDs are twice as likely to give a protocol without a cooperative response and when they do offer one it is likely to be spoiled. Interestingly, aggressive responses are twice as likely in normal males than in APD's, perhaps owing to a lessened degree of psychic conflict in regards to such behavior. In fact, those with higher psychopathy scores on the PCL-R (Hare, 1991) actually produce progressively less aggressive responses. Human detail and fantasized human objects dominate the intrapsychic world of the APD with whole human responses much less prevalent than in normal samples.

Self-Perception

Almost half of APD's produce an impaired egocentricity index. They are more likely to produce morbid responses, but only half as likely to produce an FD response. Approximately 35 percent of APD's will produce at least one reflection response, with the number and prevalence of these responses increasing with greater levels of assessed psychopathy. This is due to a more smoothly functioning grandiosity and less conflicted sense of self among more psychopathic subjects.

Ideation

The cognitive processes of the APD can easily resemble a more seriously thought disordered subject even in the absence of intentional exaggeration. Among ideational responses M-responses, rare in normals, become quite commonplace. The sum of special scores also tends to show elevations, though there is a high degree of variability in this measure amongst APD's. Particularly among those with greater assessed psychopathy, there is a tendency to display less inclination to delay action in order to gather further data before proceeding with a behavioral response (as measured by $p>a+1$).

Mediation

A lack of perceptual convergence is the norm with APD's (in 85% of cases X+%<70). This occurs in the presence or absence of other thoughts or emotions (in 80% of cases F+%<70). Reality testing is often found to be functioning at the borderline level of impairment for

61 percent of APD's and at the psychotic level for 18 percent. APD's tend to produce fewer popular responses than normals as well.

Processing

APD's are more likely to be underincorporative (26% vs. 5% of norms). They also tend to give almost five times as many Dd responses as seen in normal subjects. The aspiration ratio of the typical APD is at the grandiose level.

MINNESOTA MULTIPHASIC PERSONALITY INVENTORY (MMPI)

Research on Detecting Malingering with the MMPI/MMPI-2

The original validity scales of the MMPI have been maintained on the MMPI-2, with three new validity scales added in the development of the revised version (Butcher et al., 1989). Although the L, F, and K scales were maintained on the MMPI-2, some items were deleted from the F scale and some items were reworded on all three scales. New validity scales include the Fb (the back side F), the True Response Inconsistency (TRIN) and the Variable Response Inconsistency (VRIN) scales. The Fb is quite similar to the F, but includes only items from the latter part of the test booklet. The TRIN and VRIN are inconsistency scales designed to identify random responding. Comparable results on the validity scales in assessments of malingering have been reported between the MMPI and MMPI-2 (Graham, Watts, & Timbrook, 1991). In addition to these scales the Infrequency Scale for Psychopathology, or F(p), has received some positive attention in recent studies of malingering (Arbisi & Ben-Porath, 1995).

Examinees attempting to malinger symptoms of mental illness can vary from rather crude attempts to fake a generic psychopathological condition to rather sophisticated attempts to fake a specific diagnostic entity. Crude attempts at generic deception are readily detected by a number of MMPI and MMPI-2 scales (Nichols & Greene, 1997) including F, F(b), F-K (Gough, 1950), and Ds (Gough, 1954). More sophisticated attempts at faking circumscribed diagnostic conditions or symptoms can be fairly difficult to detect, especially when the examinee has some knowledge of the validity indicators of the test (Lamb et al., 1994; Wetter et al., 1993). More positively for our purposes, perhaps, is that the MMPI has shown a strong ability to detect malingering of more severe psychopathological conditions such as schizophrenia (Rogers & Chakraborty, 1993; Wetter et al., 1993) and borderline personality disorder (Sivec et al., 1995; Wetter et al., 1994). The malingering of disorders such as depression, which are more universally experienced and understood by the general population, are more difficult to detect (Bagby et al., 1997). Generally speaking, in forensic examinations of inmates, it is the more severe psychotic conditions in which we are asked to confirm or deny their existence. In the following review, therefore, we will focus our attention on studies of malingering that have involved attempts to fake psychotic conditions with particular emphasis on investigations which have used inmates as subjects.

Berry, Baer and Harris (1991), in their meta-analysis of MMPI malingering research, found that T-scaled and raw F indices had the highest absolute effect sizes across studies with the F-K index close behind. They also noted that research which gave participants global "fake bad" instructions produced larger differences from normal protocols than when malingerers were attempting to fake a specific clinical syndrome. This would imply that cut-off scores established from research which focuses on those malingering specific illnesses should translate into appropriate decisions for those faking more non-specific disturbance, but not the reverse.

Rogers, Bagby and Chakraborty (1993) examined the ability of community subjects to simulate schizophrenic symptoms on the MMPI-2 after being instructed on the symptoms of schizophrenia or on test strategies for detecting malingerers. These groups were compared to groups instructed in both aspects of malingering, schizophrenic inpatients and to an uncoached group also asked to malinger psychosis. Those attempting malingering were offered a monetary incentive for successfully escaping detection. Results showed that the F and F-K scales misclassified one-third of those given information on schizophrenic symptoms and those given no information to assist in their efforts to malinger, and performed even more poorly on subjects given information on psychometric strategies for detecting malingering. The authors found that the Ds and the Wiener-Harmon Subtle-Obvious (S-O) scales (Wiener, 1948) were each able to identify two-thirds of those coached on test detection strategies as well as 80 percent of other types of malingerers. Overall, the authors found that information on test detection strategies was more useful to potential malingerers than knowledge of schizophrenia. In fact, those given both types of information were not as effective in their efforts to deceive as those given just knowledge of test detection strategies alone. The usefulness of the S-O scales in this study is an anomaly in the midst of numerous studies that have found no discriminant validity of the scales in distinguishing true from malingered protocols (Bagby et al., 1997; Bagby et al., 1995; Timbrook et al., 1993; Weed, Ben-Porath, & Butcher, 1990).

Bagby et al. (1997) offered undergraduate psychology students rewards for successfully simulating either schizophrenia or depression. Students were given information about the disorder to be simulated prior to being administered the MMPI-2. Their results were then compared to a reference sample of actual patients with the disorder. Participants feigning schizophrenia scored significantly higher on all of the validity scales and indicators than did patients with schizophrenia. The largest effect sizes in distinguishing malingerers from true schizophrenics were for F, F-K, F(p), and F(b), respectively. Table 6.1 summarizes the mean raw score results across the two groups on these scales.

Several studies have assessed the general utility of using the MMPI in detecting malingering with prison inmates. Hunt (1948) found the F-K useful in differentiating the MMPI protocols of 74 Navy courts-martial prisoners asked to complete a series of MMPI's in which they first responded honestly, then were instructed to fake good and then to fake bad. Walters, White and Greene (1988) found that the F, F-K and Ds scales all successfully differentiated penitentiary inmates motivated to appear mentally ill to support their requests for single cell placements from inmates undergoing parole evaluations (denial condition) and inmates voluntarily entering group therapy (neutral condition).

Grossman and Wasyliw (1988) compared a group of inmates under evaluation with the claim of being not guilty of their crimes by reason of insanity (NGRI) with a group of inmates that had already successfully pleaded their cases in this manner. Presumably, the group still under evaluation would have reason to exaggerate their problems while the other would not. The authors found that the test was, indeed, sensitive to this condition with 14 percent to 41 percent of examinees clearly indicated as malingering according to the measure used. Wasyliw et al. (1988) conducted a similar comparison and found the Ds scale to be especially sensitive to the malingering of potential NGRI testees, probably due to their crude tendency to exaggerate all problems, rather than overemphasize disorder-specific symptomatology. The authors also found F to be a better indicator of malingering in this study than F-K.

TABLE 6.1
MEANS AND STANDARD DEVIATIONS OF RAW VALIDITY
SCORES ON MMPI-2 COMPARISON OF STUDENTS FEIGNING
SCHIZOPHRENIA WITH ACTUAL SCHIZOPHRENIC PATIENTS
(BAGBY ET AL., 1997).

Scale	Students Feigning Illness	Schizophrenic Group
F	42.3 (7.7)	12.1 (77)
Fb	24.9 (8.2)	9.3 (6.9)
F-K	32.5 (11.2)	-2.3 (10.3)
F(p)	15.4 (4.4)	3.0 (2.7)

Iverson, Franzen, and Hammond (1995) compared the protocols of 55 minimum security inmates given general fake-bad instructions to 51 non-criminal inpatients on MMPI-2. Using a cut-off score of 17 on the F scale, 89 percent of malingerers were correctly identified with only 2 percent of actual patients being misclassified. F-K classified 86 percent of malingerers with a 2 percent misclassification rate of patients with a cut-off score of 9. F(b) displayed a poorer discriminant validity. Using the maximally effective cut-off score of 18, only 61 percent of malingerers were so identified with 4 percent of patients misclassified.

Hawk and Cornell (1989) compared samples of malingering, psychotic and non-psychotic criminal defendants undergoing forensic evaluations on the MMPI. Interestingly, they also found that 50 percent of both the psychotic and malingering groups gave incomplete or random responses which rendered the test unusable. However, they did find that the malingering group scored significantly higher on both F and F-K when valid protocols were obtained.

Schretlen and Arkowitz (1990) measured the ability of a psychological test battery to differentiate inmates asked to fake insanity from groups of non-criminal psychiatric patients and inmate controls. Detection of malingering was attempted with use of the Bender Gestalt, a Malingering scale composed of IQ items that most examinees would be expected to pass and the F and F-K indices of the MMPI. The best single discriminator of faking was found to be the F scale raw score which detected 80 percent of malingerers with only 10 percent false positives. Use of the battery of tests together was able to identify 85 percent of malingerers with no false positives.

Kurtz (1993) found the MMPI-2 F, F-K and Fb scales able to detect malingering of prison inmates instructed to fake psychosis after either being given didactic information on schizophrenia or being instructed to role play another individual genuinely suffering from psychiatric illness. Similar to Schretlen and Arkowitz (1990), this study found that additional sources of information (SIRS and M test) contributed to the ability to detect malingering when other sources of MMPI-2 profile validity needed to be ruled out.

Recommended cut-off scores for detecting malingering on the F and F-K scales, the most commonly evaluated and supported, vary across studies. Butcher et al. (1991) recommended a F cut-off score of 11. Graham, Watts and Timbrook found 23 to be most useful. Among sophisticated malingerers Rogers, Bagby and Chakraborty (1993) found a cut-off of 28 necessary. Schretlen and Arkowitz (1990) found that an F-K cut-off of 11 and an F raw score cut-off of 19 most effectively differentiated inmate malingerers from inmate controls. The recommended cut-off scores increased to 17 and 26, respectively, when differentiating between inmate malingerers and non-criminal psychiatric patients. It would seem appropriate to apply the more stringent cut-off's to the most sophisticated and motivated malingerers with lesser scores required for other populations.

A less common validity indicator that is useful in detecting crude attempts at malingering which involve indiscriminate endorsements of psychopathological symptoms has been outlined by Levitt and Gotts (1995). They have suggested using the Mean Elevation (ME) of the eight clinical scales (Scales 1-4 and 6-8). For normals, ME is typically in the range of 45-55T. For general psychiatric inpatients and outpatients, the range increases to 55-65T. Profiles of the most severely distressed psychiatric patients rarely exceed an ME of 80T. An ME exceeding 85T, therefore, strongly suggests an overinclusive endorsement of psychopathological symptoms in a crude attempt at simulating the existence of mental illness.

An additional validity indicator of crude attempts at malingering is the percentage of responses answered in the true direction (True %). Most MMPI/MMPI-2 items indicative of psychopathology are keyed in the true direction. Thus, indiscriminant endorsement of symptoms will result in a high True percent. As True percent increases, high elevations are likely to occur on scales F, 6, 8, and 9. On the MMPI-2, some degree of deception is suggested whenever the True percent reaches a level of 60 (Nichols & Greene, 1997).

Studies reviewed show the MMPI and MMPI-2 to be powerful tools in efforts to distinguish individuals trying to malinger mental disorder. It would appear that up to 80 percent of malingerers can be effectively identified with few false positives occurring. In actual clinical practice, use of the MMPI in isolation would be rare. Thus, the addition of other instruments to detect deceptive intent of examinees should be expected to result in an extremely high ability to discern the validity of examinees psychological complaints.

Code Type Interpretation With the MMPI-2

The question of whether it is best to utilize the MMPI or MMPI-2 in forensic evaluations has been a persistent concern since the introduction of the revised edition. While the updated item pool and improved normative sample of the MMPI-2 are desirable improvements over the original edition, the substantial body of empirical knowledge compounded on the original version may not fully apply to the new form of the test. This is a particularly poignant concern given data such as that the same set of raw scores from the two tests can lead to entirely different codings of T scores, profile configurations and code-type interpretations (Humphrey & Dahlstrom, 1995). In fact, one-third of clinical examinees who belong to one MMPI-2 code type will belong to a different MMPI code type (Butcher et al., 1989), and as many as 60 percent of 2-point code type members in the normal range on one profile may not belong to the same grouping on the other profile (Dahlstrom, 1992). In fact, the MMPI-2 manual describes 21.5 percent of a sample of 423 psychiatric cases as producing profiles in the normal range, while only 8 percent were in the normal range when plotted on traditional MMPI profiles.

Caldwell (1997) has called for use of the MMPI-2 booklet with a double plotting of the raw score results. The contemporary MMPI-2 profile can be examined on a scale-by-scale normative basis while the MMPI profile can be used to access the 50-plus years of pattern research available on that instrument. He has also suggested that this is not a difficult practice to defend in court. Juries and judges are able to understand the need to update the items from a test 60 years old while accepting the usefulness of 50 years of pattern research compared to a paucity of such on the MMPI-2. As this is now standard and accepted practice, it is actually considerably more risky to not follow such recommendations in clinical and forensic practice.

The Megargee Scales

Megargee and Bohn (1977 1979) outlined an empirically-based comprehensive system for classifying youthful offenders based on responses to the MMPI. Ten offender "types" resulted, each with its own descriptors and characteristics (Megargee, 1984). Although the Megargee types have been found to generalize to other correctional settings (Carey, Garske, & Ginsberg, 1986; Hutton, Miner, & Langfeldt, 1993; Wrobel, Calovini, & Martin, 1991), its generalizability has been inconsistent (Kennedy, 1986), with particular problems in accurately classifying black inmates (Carey, Garske, & Ginsberg, 1986; Hutton & Miner, 1995). Some studies have questioned the temporal stability of the types, noting 60-90 percent changes in type in as little as a 4-month period (Dahlstrom et al., 1986; Johnson, Simmons, & Gordon, 1983; Simmons et al., 1981). Some authors have suggested, however, that such changes may reflect genuine alterations in inmate perspective/functioning (Zager, 1988).

Some studies have found the typology to be useful in predicting and managing inmate populations. Voorhis (1988) demonstrated clear correlations between the Megargee Types and expected levels of disciplinary infractions. Wright (1988) found the typology to be predictive of self-reported problems in an inmate's ability to effectively relate to other inmates and staff members. The typology has been successfully used in a Federal facility to reduce institutional violence by segregating predatory and assaultive inmates from those most likely to be exploited and victimized (Bohn, 1979).

Zager (1988) concluded that type descriptors have consistently generalized across settings for 7 of the 10 types. Predicting adjustment based on the types has been inconsistent, however, which may be due to serious methodological flaws in studies to date. The better studies available seem to provide some support for the usefulness of the typology. Kennedy (1986) concluded in his review of the literature that studies have not shown the typology to be effective as a predictor of inmate violence or aggression during incarceration. At this point in time it may be quite hard to defend a reliance on results based on this system for substantial interpretive or predictive reasons. Until further validation and/or refinement of the Megargee System use of the types in forensic evaluations should probably be confined to being utilized as a source of additional hypotheses about the case in question which can be confirmed or disconfirmed from other information sources.

The Overcontrolled-Hostility (0-H) Scale

The Overcontrolled-Hostility (O-H) Scale was developed by Megargee, Cook and Mendelsohn (1967) as a predictor of assaultiveness among prison inmates. The authors wished to identify individuals who were chronically overcontrolled in their expression of aggression such that they might act out in an extremely aggressive manner at times. The 31-item O-H scale is composed of items that were differentially endorsed by extremely assaultive prison inmates, assaultive inmates, inmates convicted of non-violent crimes and men who had never been convicted of crimes. A high score corresponds to a more overcontrolled, assaultive person. Applicability of the scale in predicting assaultiveness of examinees has not been established, and some difficulties in cross-validation and applicability to black inmates has been noted (Hutton, Miner, Blades, & Langfeldt, 1992). High scores may suggest some explanation for extreme assaultiveness when this behavior has been otherwise demonstrated. As with the Megargee types, then, one should be most cautious in attempting use for clinical and/or forensic purposes. The Megargee typology and the O-H scale may, however, be a rich source of research investigation and a more direct clinical utility in the future.

THE MILLON INVENTORIES

The Millon Clinical Multiaxial Inventories (MCMI) provide forced choice items designed to facilitate the diagnosis and description of psychiatric patients (Millon, 1977, 1981, 1987, 1994). The Millon Inventories have gained considerable success both nationally (Piotrowski & Keller, 1989; Piotrowski & Lubin, 1989, 1990) and internationally (Lutejn, 1990; Simonsen & Mortensen, 1990) in recent years. Additionally, they have gained increasing prevalence and acceptance in the courtroom (McCann & Dyer, 1996) and have demonstrated some ability to detect malingered protocols (Bagby, Gillis & Dickens, 1990). Nevertheless, use of the MCMI for forensic evaluations is not recommended at this time for several reasons.

While the MCMI may give additional insights into the Axis II disorders that are commonly encountered in the correctional setting and is more closely aligned with the DSM-IV, it is more difficult to defend in the courtroom in the face of a particularly aggressive lawyer. First, the plethora of research available on the MMPI dwarfs that of the MCMI and the two provide a great deal of redundant information in their results and in their data collection method. Second, there is some degree of static in the composition and organization of the MCMI with the third edition appearing in 1994, the second in 1987 and the first in 1977. While many studies may find results of earlier editions transferable to later ones, this cannot be assumed and will not be empirically validated until a single edition is allowed sufficient opportunity to be studied and described as to its idiosyncratic strengths and weaknesses. An additional problem with the MCMI is that it is both a theory-driven test as well as an empirical one. While this may be a strength in some respects, it is the empirical aspect of a test that is of utmost importance to its use in applied settings.

Without the requisite empirical data to support interpretative descriptions, theoretical data must be used with a degree of caution. In a given test administration, the test interpretations offered by computer-based and cookbook sources offer phrases derived from Millons (1981) descriptions of the diagnosis that is most likely applicable given the test results. This is in contrast to tests such as the MMPI, for example, in that the test interpretations are usually empirically validated phrases and statements directly related to the test items. This results in two problems for the users of the MCMI. First, the additional interpretive step introduces an additional opportunity for error to arise in the interpretive summary. Second, as ones interpretive description becomes more "rich" it becomes increasingly less clear what the direct source of any individual interpretive statement is. Third, it introduces the possibility of an interpretive statement that matches the test-related diagnosis, but may be incompatible with an item-level test result. If your interpretation states that patient X is afraid of crowds, for example, but the same patient responded false to this at the item level of the test, you could have an embarrassingly difficult time defending your data in court.

The most difficult task for the MCMI user in court will be to explain the test construction and interpretation process to a layperson jury. With the MMPI one needs only to indicate that statements provided are empirically derived correlates of test results at the profile, scale or item level. With the MCMI, one has the added burden of explaining Millon's theory of personality disorders (as eloquent as it might be), the empirical underpinnings of the test itself and how the two come together. I suspect that any bright lawyer with adequate preparation could cause this discussion to become so convoluted as to render any subsequent testimony regarding the results relation to the case to be lost, if not outright ignored. It is without a doubt a promising instrument whose place in the courtroom may, in time, come to make it a more formidable opponent to the MMPI. But at this time, it is its' susceptibility to legal attack (some of which may be quite reasonable and valid), that I believe make the MCMI not quite ready to dethrone the MMPI in forensic evaluations.

USE OF INTELLIGENCE TESTS TO DETECT MALINGERING

Use of intelligence tests to detect malingering emanates from efforts to detect potential military draftees efforts to malinger mental deficiency in order to avoid military conscription. The predominance of studies performed have been to detect either mental retardation or neurological disturbance (Hunt & Older, 1943; Goldstein, 1945; Hunt, 1946; Crowley, 1952; Pollaczek, 1952; Heaton et al., 1978; Goebel, 1983). There has been some evidence accrued from other studies, however, that similar strategies can be used to detect malingering in subjects attempting to feign schizophrenia (Wachspress, Beren-berg, & Jacobson, 1953; Anderson, Trethowan, & Kenna, 1965; Bash & Alpert, 1980; Schretlen, 1986). The actual test instruments utilized have also varied, but enough have incorporated the WAIS to conclude that findings are consistent across tests.

With regards to performing a forensic evaluation in a case of suspected malingering, the target for the malingerer is most often to establish psychosis with a diagnosis of schizophrenia. A large number of people operate under the mistaken assumption that schizophrenics are quite similar in functioning to retardates. Malingerers, however, are often unsure of what information a retardate or crazy person should know and how much. As a result, much of the types of responses that were significant in detecting malingering with the Rorschach will also be significant with an intelligence test such as the WAIS-IV (Wechsler, 2008). A malingerer might refuse to cooperate sufficiently for the test to be administered at all, though they do not appear as dramatically disturbed as a true schizophrenic would be who was unable to complete the testing. Malingerers might also exhibit forced expressions of perplexity over test directions or miss easy and obvious items. They may also exhibit prolonged response times or excessive pauses before offering test responses. Overall scores for a malingerer, if they associate "craziness" with intellectual impairment, are likely to be significantly below estimates based on their level of education, general functioning and other demographic factors, as well as below scores obtained by typical psychotic patients (Schretlen, 1986).

The most consistently applied and useful method of objectively assessing malingering on standardized intelligence tests has been to examine intratest "scatter." That is, malingerers have been found to be much more likely to fail more easy test items while passing more hard items than those giving a more honest presentation (Crowley, 1952; Hunt & Older, 1943; Goldstein, 1945). This result has been most prevalent in tests where items are not hierarchicly arranged as they are on the WAIS-IV so that the level of difficulty for individual items is less obvious. Nevertheless, one might expect greater intratest and intertest scatter with a malingering subject even on the WAIS-IV. In cases of suspected malingering one could also opt to substitute or augment the assessment with a test other than the WAIS-IV that has more utility in measuring this factor. Schretlen (1986), for example, has composed an instrument made up of intelligence test items that are arranged in random order that might be a useful adjunct. Malingerers are also more likely to offer bizarre responses to even simple test questions and to offer approximate responses. In the latter instance, subjects offer responses that are wrong, but close enough to being correct as to imply knowledge of the information in question. Bash and Alpert

(1980) have operationalized the measurement of approximate answers to six tests of the WAIS that was demonstrated to differentiate malingerers from psychotic and non-psychotic controls.

Detection of malingering across the studies outlined herein found that the accurate identification of malingering was possible in approximately 80-90 percent of cases. Using the various techniques identified in each study together should produce comparable, if not improved, results. Thus, the use of intelligence testing can serve to provide an accurate intellectual assessment in true cases of mental illness and an additional tool for detecting feigned mental illness in subjects who malinger.

SUMMARY

Strategies with strong empirical support have been developed to detect attempts at malingering mental illness through numerous means. The overall ability of clinical interviews and psychological tests to detect malingering appears to be quite good for each of several measures. Despite the demonstrated ability of these measures, no single strategy is foolproof. Given the rather great importance the outcome of an examination of this nature may have on the examinee, one should always be careful to use multiple points of data in cases where clear evidence of malingering has not been obtained. One of the greatest tools in carrying out such evaluations involves looking for consistency across tests and interviews which can be quite difficult to maintain by a malingerer over substantial periods of time and across varying situations. There are times when a malingering examinee may be able to foil one method, but reveal their charade when tested in another manner. An examinee that presents as mentally retarded on an intelligence test, for example, would be expected to have some difficulty reading items on the MMPI and to show a less than sophisticated approach to the Rorschach. The use of a test battery in the most difficult cases of suspected malingering should be sufficient to allow confident determinations of the veracity of psychopathological reports of examinees.

Chapter 7

ESTABLISHING AND MAINTAINING APPROPRIATE RELATIONSHIPS WITH CORRECTIONAL STAFF

IT CAN EASILY SEEM AT TIMES that dealing with inmates is the easier part of your professional responsibilities in a correctional environment, while maintaining positive relationships with staff is the more difficult and time-consuming. One does become hardened to some degree towards inmates such that their more trivial problems and manipulations can, when necessary, be summarily dismissed and/or ignored in the interest of dealing with more pressing concerns. It is not so easy when it is a staff member creating or presenting problems.

Staff perceptions of psychologists run the gamut from appreciation and respect to disdain, disrespect and even outright paranoia. Those at the lower staff positions within the institution often have the least understanding of what it is we do in the institution. They may be reluctant to call on us in appropriate situations and/or inappropriately refer to us on others because of this general lack of understanding of our role and some discomfort about being involved in any way with a mental health professional. After all, we are dealing with law enforcement professionals here. These people, as a class, do not have a strong tendency or even willingness to call upon help from others except within the tight confines of performing their assigned tasks within the parameters they are trained to (e.g., calling for backup in dealing with an assaultive inmate). When it comes to psychologists, not only are they very unlikely to ask for personal assistance when they may need it, but many of them appear fearful of even being seen talking to the staff psychologist out of some paranoia that they will be perceived by other staff as having "problems." It is, thus, more difficult to establish positive trusting relationships with other staff members, though other reasons further complicate the problem.

As in any large work environment, with the majority of people you interact with you will encounter few problems or complications and will probably work more in parallel with them as opposed to working in direct collaboration or conflict. Additionally, there will be that small minority that will take up an inordinate amount of time and patience because of their idiosyncratic personality quirks or a lack of congruence with your own style of interacting with the world. Generally speaking, correctional staff probably have a greater tendency than most to work cooperatively with others, at least in the face of crisis or difficult situations.

Staff members are your lifeline within the institution. They will not only willingly come to your aid in the event of some physical threat to your well-being, but can make your job considerably easier in many instances if you have cultivated the proper relationship with them. As a psychologist in this setting, you will likely have hundreds of inmates to monitor which means you will have a very limited contact with any one of them. As discussed in Chapter 4 on inmate relations, infrequent contact with individual inmates, coupled with your ability to listen and empathize with others' difficulties, can make you a prime target of inmate manipulation. It is surprising, though, that even the best manipulators oftentimes return to normalcy as soon as they leave our office. By taking the time to talk to other staff members that see them in the housing units, recreation yard, assigned job site, etc., you will sometimes be amazed at the remarkable contrast in inmate behaviors that occur between your office and the rest of the compound. Communication with other staff is often a key means of avoiding inmate manipulations and properly assessing inmates institutional adjustment and/or treatment progress.

In speaking with staff about particular inmates, it is obvious that some staff are more cognizant of abnormalities or affective difficulties of those around them than others, so it is important not to place too much weight on any one staff's assessment. These are, after all, laypersons. However, it has been my experience that the majority of staff members, when questioned, can give you a fairly accurate assessment of an inmate they've had contact with concerning general demeanor, mood, and behavior. Their assessment of the underlying motivations for unusual behavior is often erroneous and naive, giving tendency to want to hold inmates responsible for all behaviors, not give them any excuses, and to see all inmates as manipulative. In terms of base rates, it is probably wise to assume that all unusual behavior is merely inmate manipulation as one would be right the vast majority of the time. However, as mental health professionals we are present in the institution and paid to individually and professionally assess each situation and I believe we can significantly exceed the success ratio of base rates if we use the tools available to us, even in this environment.

Another method of assessing inmates in cases of questionable validity or greater importance for an accurate judgment (such as in forensic responsibility assessments) is to directly observe them yourself on the compound. Also discussed in Chapter 4, this makes one appear far more approachable and interested in the inmates' welfare, gives one an opportunity to objectively assess the true level of functioning of specific inmates in environments outside the psychologists office and it also places one in contact with staff members, enabling one to cultivate these relationships at the same time. Your presence outside your own "turf" can help staff perceive you as one of them and as committed to the overall goals of the institution.

EMPLOYEE ASSISTANCE PROGRAMS

Within many correctional facilities, psychologists are asked as part of their responsibilities to also intervene in employee assistance matters. These duties usually rest upon the quite shaky assumption that those in need of help will voluntarily seek it and the psychologist, being a familiar figure to the employee, will be easier to approach for such assistance. Sometimes, this actually occurs and can be a positive experience for the employee and a benefit to the institution as a whole. Oftentimes, the process is prostituted to the possible detriment of the employee and the institution, as well as the definite detriment of the psychologist. Let me say that I do not think the problem of having the on-site psychologist double as an EAP provider is specific to the correctional environment. It was my experience working with the VA system, for example, that similar problems occurred there and my inter-

actions with colleagues suggest this occurs in many other occupational environments as well. Within the correctional system, however, it
serves as a further complication to the already complicated process of
nurturing positive and trusting relationships with staff members.

One of the difficulties is that instead of being self-referred, many of
those one sees in the EAP are forcefully referred by supervisors at the
institution. These supervisors are often your administrative supervisors as well. In spite of your insistence and persistence in informing
these individuals of the "voluntary" nature of the EAP and the inap-
propriateness of forced referrals, they will often continue to come.
Additionally, because these supervisors had reason to refer their
employees to you in the first place, they typically will want to know
what your assessment and recommendations were of the employee.
The fact that this tears asunder rules of confidentiality is usually appreciated only by you. Obviously, you would not violate the limits of confidentiality in this situation unless the usual exceptions of dangerous-
ness and such were present, however, with the employee's permission,
you can speak to the referring party openly. It does not take a great
leap of intelligence to further understand that an employee who was
forcefully referred to you by their supervisor is going to feel great pressure in signing a release form for you to speak to their bosses, because
they often feel the alternative is greater friction or punitive action. This
is not all that different, in practice, from a police officer being called
in to referee a domestic dispute in a residential setting. Just as domestic calls are often the most anxiety-provoking and dangerous situations
for police 'officers and may trigger their stress reactions more than
other calls, so should your inner alarm bells ring when an EAP request
comes in from a supervisor on one of their employees. In some cases,
forced EAP referrals can be minimized by training administrative staff
on the purpose and appropriate use of the EAP. In other cases, though,
this training will have little effect.

The problem that existed between the supervisor and supervisee
may be one of brief duration and isolated occurrence. They may come
to largely forget the problem and bury any negative feelings towards
one another over the incident. Unfortunately, negative feelings
towards the psychologist will often be one result of the situation, and
these feelings will not be so easily discharged. In fact, it often produces
a degree of disdain and paranoia towards the psychologist from the
person referred for EAP assistance. These feelings do not tend to be

openly expressed in the correctional environment in which we work. Instead, they are expressed in subtle, often passive aggressive ways. Dealing with the case manager, unit manager, personnel officer or whatever position the employee occupies will from then on be an exercise in patience and determination. In some cases, long-term efforts to build a friendly, relaxed relationship with the staff member can serve to mitigate the problem. In many others, nothing you do will ever result in your being trusted or that employee being in any hurry to cooperate in working with you in appropriately dealing with the inmate population. To say that these problems could be circumvented by eliminating the institutional psychologists role in the EAP process is naive, however.

EFFECT OF STAFF CONTACT WITH MENTAL HEALTH SERVICES ON PERCEPTIONS OF PSYCHOLOGY

Correctional staff, in general, are focused on the inadequacies of others and do not tend to be greatly interested in self-evaluations and self-understanding. Oftentimes, those that end up before mental health professionals will be unsuccessful in gaining significant benefit from these interactions and will often blame the psychologist for the treatment failure, as well as for making them feel demeaned by the process of coming before a mental health worker to begin with. After all, therapy is a power relationship at its core – the patient is to some degree acknowledging an inability to direct some aspect of their life and the therapist is seen as having the ability and knowledge the patient lacks. Correctional workers are loathe to concede control to others, both because of their preexisting personality characteristics and the tendency to become more controlling from working in the correctional environment. This presents negative feelings and distrust towards the therapist and a much greater likelihood of treatment failure, which in turn increases initial negative feelings towards the therapist and disdain for the profession as a whole.

As one common example, consider the correctional worker who deals with the stresses of correctional work by spending much of their free time interacting with peers from the correctional environment and engaging in relatively heavy use of alcohol. They may share little of their feelings and problems with family members and their need to maintain a quiet, orderly environment through personal control may eventually create increasingly greater conflicts within their family or increasing emotional distancing from family members. Eventually, the spouse of the correctional officer demands that he participate in marriage counseling. The officer, though feeling it unnecessary and coerced, nonetheless reluctantly agrees, seeing no other real option, for refusal may lead to divorce and loss of family. Within the counseling sessions, the officer may be unable to open up or acknowledge their personal contribution to the problems they are experiencing, with counseling eventually being terminated and labeled unsuccessful. This scenario is obviously not pure science fiction, but is played out on a regular basis with both correctional officers and others. The point to be made here is how it comes to affect the correctional officers perception of the institution psychologist. First, they harbor anger over having been forced to see a therapist. Second, they feel belittled by having engaged in a relationship in which they were forced to give up personal control. Third, they perceive their marriage counseling as a complete waste of time, blame the psychologist for the treatment failure and find it to provide confirming evidence of the uselessness of psychology as a profession.

The negative feelings engendered against the psychologist are subconsciously transferred to you, such that you will then be treated with contempt and never understand why. I guarantee that you will have employees that you will be quite convinced this process is playing itself out just by their reactions to you. If there are any reasons why we as psychologists should want to remain involved in the EAP process, I suppose this is one. After all, if someone is going to be forced into treatment in some way and hate me for the rest of my life, I would like to at least be aware of why they detest me so much, rather than merely inheriting their feelings from their past treatment involvements. I also probably don't need to remind you that there are some psychologists with whom I would prefer not to be associated with and about which I might have to defend the patient in their complaints against the therapist. The bottom line is I would like to maintain as much control over how others perceive me and my profession as possible (the control objective of correctional employees demonstrated anew!). Of course, the flip side of the situation is true as well. You will, on occasion, get an employee who will voluntarily seek you out for legitimate reasons, be helped by your interventions, and be appreciative of your efforts. Obviously, this employee can smooth the way towards accomplishing your objectives within the work setting from then on because they have developed a true and accurate appreciation of what you do and the benefits it can have. For better or worse, the EAP process is rife with contradictions, complexities, dualities of relationships and complications.

To avoid some of the pitfalls, I would encourage anyone in this field to be willing to approach staff members they observe to appear depressed or who are known to have recently been going through difficult circumstances, divorce, family death or illness, etc. These informal approaches can give staff members an opportunity to talk to someone about their problems who is willing to listen, without having to claim or appear to be unable to handle their problems independently. They maintain their dignity and pride, while being able to lift some of the emotional burden within them. In fact, such contact can benefit you as well. Since you are engaging in friendly conversation, the various paperwork requirements which would have been required of a formal EAP contact, can be circumvented. You can open the door for that employee to engage in further contact with you on a formal or informal nature, build a positive relationship with them and perhaps provide a modicum of education as to the value your services can offer. I guarantee if you find yourself in trouble later you may find yourself surprised as to how fast people you approached in this manner come running to assist you.

Staff Perceptions of Inmate Responsibility

It is an unfortunate fact, perhaps, but throughout your duties as a correctional psychologist you will find that the custodial staff have little understanding of what it is you do as a psychologist and even lesser understanding of how you do it. In fact, the little understanding they do have is usually quite contrary to reality. As a result, it is often when you are least felt to be needed that you are most called for in the situation and vice versa. Consider the case of a mentally ill inmate who suffers a psychotic episode during which he assaults another inmate or threatens to assault a staff member in anger. From the point of view of the custodial staff, this inmate needs to be punished, and they are loathe to hear a psychologist proclaim that the inmate should not be held responsible for any misbehavior. Realistically, it is rare that an inmate will be excused for misbehavior in this manner and as well it should be rare. However, there do arise cases where this defense is a legitimate issue and in such cases, forcing a distressed mentally ill inmate to be in seclusion for 30-60 days as punishment can have serious deleterious consequences on his mental health and, ultimately, how safe it is for him to be returned to the general population.

The prevalent and fixed perception of staff members to inmates judged to be incompetent for their actions is that they are therefore automatically excused forevermore from any negative behaviors they engage in. You will commonly hear staff members incredulously lament, "He can go out and kill somebody if he wants to and then just say he wasn't responsible for what he did." Although this may seem a very simplistic view, it is nevertheless common and emanates from basic misperceptions regarding the association between mental illness and criminal conduct among the general public. In reality, the judgment that the individual is not responsible for his actions is confined to the situation at hand and does not provide a blanket release of responsibility for actions before or after the incident in question. It is possible, perhaps even common, that the individual may have been reasonably rational and fully responsible for his behavior and decisions the day before and the day after the incident. Additionally, in such cases, the judgment of being not responsible typically will come from the psychologist who will know from observing the situation and/or events immediately before or after that the inmate was seriously disturbed cognitively. If an inmate is cognizant enough to request that the psychologist release them from responsibility, chances are they were not incompetent. In fact, even after events have calmed down, the truly incompetent will usually remain separated from their environment enough that they will be unconcerned and/or unaware of the potential consequences they face or may be more concerned about the problems they caused than what will happen to them as a result. Both reactions, when genuine, would seem to bolster the argument that the inmate was truly incapacitated at the time.

As an example of what I felt to be a legitimate case of not being responsible, I recall a case of an individual that was being maintained in a one-man maximum security cell. In such an environment, he was allowed to come out of his cell for only one hour of recreational activities per day and to be escorted to take a shower two times per week. He had been maintained in this environment for some time and did not see an end to this environmental seclusion in his future. Partly out of desperation and probably also as an attention-getting move, he attempted to hang himself in his cell. He was discovered rather soon into the attempt so that he was actually suspended for only a matter of minutes, but did lose consciousness and managed to produce a rather nasty-looking mark on his neck that undoubtedly gave him a major sore throat. I visited the inmate in the hospital approximately two hours after the incident, during which time he spoke with me far more than he ever had before or ever would in the future. He was very despondent and depressed and cried through much of the interview. It is interesting that he nevertheless persisted in speaking quite openly with me, even when it was obvious that it hurt to talk because of the injuries he had sustained.

The emotion with which this inmate was dealing with were quite powerful and I must admit I was not adequately prepared at the time for it myself. It was a Friday afternoon and I had actually had to extend my tour of duty to assess the inmate, so that after visiting him in the hospital I headed immediately for home. While driving home that day I found myself weeping openly. Such an experience is hard to explain to someone outside the field in which I practice, but I think an effective therapist has the ability to feel the emotions of their client within themselves. This is a talent, I feel, which allows one to better understand the client and more effectively and sensitively deal with them. Unfortunately, however, it leaves one open to becoming physically and psychologically exhausted on occasion when faced with an individual with particularly powerful emotions. Such was the case for me this day. I did not weep out of a desire to have the inmate released from prison or have his world restructured to his satisfaction. I did not weep because I had "crossed the line" into being on the inmates side rather than the side of the correctional institution for which I worked. Instead, I cried out of need to flush my system of the powerful feelings that had just passed through me. Allowing myself this experience, I felt relieved and restored, though admittedly somewhat fatigued.

I later learned that upon being returned to the institution, this inmate apparently flew into a rage and prior to being placed in physical restraints caused some minor injuries to some of the officers escorting him. My impression was clearly that of a severely distraught individual who should not be held responsible for his actions in this particular instance. I think I can legitimately say as a professional that my judgment was not clouded by emotion, but supported by it. Staff response to my judgment was almost surprisingly muted. I think those directly involved in managing the situation that day had little argument or hard feelings with the decision. Others, neither present nor particularly knowledgeable of the circumstances, expressed their opinion that "Psychology was coddling inmates again," primarily through off-handed remarks and other passive aggressive behaviors.

As for the inmate, he came to recover over a period of days, such that his restraints were removed and he returned to premorbid levels of functioning. After a couple of more minor setbacks the inmate eventually avoided all disciplinary action for a six-month period in which he acted quite appropriately to staff members. At that point he was released to a general population environment of high security inmates. Had he not been released from responsibility for his actions, he would have received several months of disciplinary action. I feel this would have only heightened his sense of helplessness about his situation and, ultimately, created additional problems for all involved.

In other situations, you will find that an inmate has managed to convince everyone of their being mentally ill and/or dangerous except for you. Although these situations are rare, they do and will oc-cur, and if not handled delicately can seriously impair what little credibility you may have with other staff. An example of a situation I was involved with will demonstrate this point.

I once was involved with an inmate in his late twenties (Inmate Jones) who left an anonymous note on his housing unit managers office stating that "Inmate Jones is going to kill himself." The note was brought to my attention and inmate Jones was sent to my office. On interview he claimed no knowledge of the note, but admitted he was tired of living and was going to soon kill himself. The inmate had a history of Borderline Personality Disorder with manipulative suicidal gestures in the past. He put on a pretty good show that seemed to indicate the presence of depression, helplessness and a genuine desire to die. Although we were not convinced entirely of his condition, we took the precaution of putting him on suicide watch. I learned that he had been pressuring his unit staff for a transfer to another facility for which he was not eligible and there were unverified rumors that he owed another inmate money that he could not come up with. Upon being admitted to the hospital for constant observation, his demeanor changed markedly. Over the next couple of days, he seemed to be rather enjoying himself and the extra attention he was getting from both staff and inmates. Many came by to offer him encouragement and to try and talk him out of any intent to harm himself. He insisted upon being interviewed that he wished to be released from suicide watch and returned to the general population. He claimed that he still had every intention of killing himself, but that we could not prevent him from doing it forever, so we might as well go ahead and release him. He refused all offers of medication and psychotherapeutic assistance. Satisfied that the inmate showed no signs of suicidality or mental illness and convinced he must actually be fearful of returning to the compound, we released him back into the general population. The hope at that point was that he would be forced to reveal what he was afraid of to obtain protection from the staff and the real problem could be dealt with. Unfortunately, this did not occur.

When released back into general population the inmate soon dropped an additional note on himself that stated, "Inmate Jones is going to kill himself." He was referred back to psychology again. At this point he reiterated that it was only a matter of time before he took his own life and there was no way that psychology could prevent it. This time, his behavior, attitude and emotions showed absolutely no congruence with his claims. In fact, he rather resembled a child who is frustrated with not getting their way and, thus, threatens to hold their breath until they turn blue. He expressed no interest in speaking or engaging in a treatment exercise and was released back in the compound. Numerous staff began to query members of the psychology department as to whether we were aware of the situation. Clearly they were confused as to how we could be allowing an admittedly suicidal inmate to walk about the compound.

A few days later we were again summoned on the inmate and this time informed that several additional notes had been left at various places. Clearly he was trying to get as much exposure as possible to make such a nuisance of himself that something would be done. The inmate was interviewed along with the operations lieutenant on duty. He was confronted with his behavior and even the fact that one of the notes was discovered within his very own cell and that all of them clearly matched his unique style of writing. He continued to deny knowledge of them, but to admit what they said was true.

I encouraged correctional staff to treat it as a disciplinary matter, for I felt him to be of no realistic threat, but felt he should be placed in segregation for his actions. For their part, they saw it as a psychology matter and could not justify locking him up when he had not actually caused any direct damage and must be mentally ill to be doing what he was doing. The inmate was thus released back onto the compound. In the absence of anyone taking action and given that we were dealing with an inmate with Borderline Personality Disorder, he was virtually forced to up the ante. The inmate then engaged in a suicidal gesture. Just as with his earlier acting out, the gesture was quite juvenile in reality, but did place all of us in a further quandary as to what to do with him. The actual attempt involved a quite superficial cut to his upper arm that probably bled less than some pimples I've had, but it was sufficient to further convince many of his genuine desire to kill himself. At this point, it was my feeling that he should still be treated as a disciplinary problem and placed in segregation, but the correctional staff could hardly believe such a recommendation, much less cooperate with it. Having exhausted other possibilities, and obviously wary of further challenging the inmates willingness to further turn up the heat to "prove" himself, I had no other alternative but to place him on suicide watch. Again, he rather enjoyed the time spent there despite all efforts to make it uncomfortable for him. In fact, despite our instructions to staff to avoid giving him undue attention because of the manipulative nature of his acts, I think many of them ended up siding with him more than us and felt the need to try and cheer him up. The inmate was transferred after several days to a Psychiatric Hospital within the Prison System. He remained there for a couple of weeks before being transferred to another institution to continue his sentence. I don't know to this day what he said to allow himself to be transferred to another institution, rather than being returned to ours as he normally would have been. However, it is interesting to note that all of the foregoing began when his unit team refused to give him a transfer he first requested and then demanded. To say this inmate had learned how to work the system would obviously be an understatement.

Some might argue that manipulative inmates need to be taken seriously and treated as genuinely suicidal. Obviously, if your professional knowledge and familiarity with the inmate do not assure you that the inmate is not a realistic threat to himself, this line of reasoning must prevail. However, experience in a correctional system will often allow you to separate true threats from harmless malingering. Treating each type of inmate accordingly will increase the respect you command from both inmates and staff and minimize over time the number of cases of inmates trying to manipulate the system through you. Another method of dealing with malingerers that some institutions use is to place even blatant cases of manipulators on suicide watch, but to make the conditions of the suicide watch so uncomfortable that it becomes a punishment in itself, thus reducing manipulation in the process.

I have spoken to psychologists that believed in routinely placing suicidal inmates in a hard cell with no clothing, no light, no heat/air conditioning and nothing but a cement block for a bed. The inmates at that institution were reluctant to admit to feelings of depression, much less suicidal ideation. Several of them admitted to me after I arrived that they were fearful of being returned to the suicide room. While the procedure may have been useful in minimizing inmates manipulating suicide, the constitutionality of the practice of treating inmates who are purportedly distressed and suicidal in this manner are highly questionable. A successful suicide in that institution would likely have brought some of these practices to light in a manner that may have endangered the jobs of the psychologists involved. Rather than appearing to be making a practice of treating truly distraught and mentally ill inmates injudiciously, the manipulators should have been identified and treated not as suicidal, but as the disciplinary problems they were.

The point to be demonstrated in the above example is how surprisingly little stock staff members will place on the psychologists professional opinion if it deviates from their more naive perspective. The only counterbalance to sway staff into cooperating with your judgment in such cases is any goodwill and confidence that you may have previously created in them towards you. Thus, once again demonstrating the importance of good staff relations.

PSYCHOEDUCATIONAL TRAINING FOR STAFF

Another route to establishing successful relationships with staff members is to provide general services to them in a group format setting. One of the easiest is that of stress management. The environment that all correctional staff members work in is by definition accompanied by heightened stress levels because of the need to maintain vigilance towards one's environment at all times and the personal knowledge, whether maintained consciously or subconsciously, that one operates within a setting that always has a degree of danger attached to it. Additionally, the push in recent years to lower costs and reduce the number of employees within the taxpayer supported public system while at the same time seeing an ever increasing population of inmates has increased workloads and lowered morale. Correctional officers and staff, like their other law enforcement brethren, are at increased risk of alcohol abuse, marital and family problems and suicide, among others (Dollard & Winefield, 1995). Many individuals drawn to this type of work are deeply committed to it, but unable to see or accept the ways it can negatively effect them until it is too late. Good stress management programs, which alert staff to the special problems they face, educate them about general stress problems and provide practical stress management education in techniques and strategies can be quite beneficial. In addition, it can serve as a bridge to staff as to what sorts of issues psychologists deal with and how we go about it. The positive effects of such interventions "rub off" onto general impressions of the individual psychologist and the field as a whole.

Educating correctional staff about the effects of their job and counterbalancing strategies for lowering their risk of stress-related problems, burnout and interference with their private interpersonal relationships can prove very helpful to maintaining their overall physical and psychological health (Cheek, 1984). The delicacy of providing such education was outlined by Cheek and Miller (1983) who reported that correctional officers consistently rate their stress levels and physical health as good, while simultaneously reporting significantly increased rates of hypertension, ulcers, heart disease, diabetes, hypoglycemia and other stress-related health problems, as well as a divorce rate twice that of the general population. The level of personal denial in this population was further exemplified by officers reporting their job environments as very stressful in general and their co-workers as highly stressed, though they presented themselves in their verbal reports to be unscathed by it. The need for awareness by correctional officers of the unique stresses of their jobs was also confirmed by their family members in the study who often reported that the officers had become increasingly controlling, bossy, demanding, suspicious, fearful, negative, critical, cold, impersonal, self-righteous and self-justifying after taking a job in corrections. Cornelius (1994) has written an excellent resource to use as a guide for discussing stress management with correctional workers or for bibliotherapy with correctional officers.

BRIDGING THE GAP WITH CORRECTIONAL STAFF

Another important bridge to establishing and maintaining good relationships with staff members is to engage in cross-training and to make frequent visits to their work areas, so that you feel comfortable doing so and they accept it as standard practice. In essence, you become part of their world or environment, instead of mysteriously separate from it. They then begin to accept you as a fellow worker rather than as the psychologist and approaching you loses its stigma. In the event that they need services in the future, they will be much more comfortable coming to you and they will also be much more willing to talk freely with you in the event you inquire about their knowledge of the functioning or circumstances of an individual inmate. I have found it not only important to attempt to engage in such practice on a regular occasion, but also have found that there is a great degree of variability in how long one of these "visits" last. On some days I may be able to visit numerous areas and make superficial and quick contacts with many different staff members. On other days I may get stopped in the first or second area visited for a lengthy discussion of personal or non-personal issues. It is important to remember in such situations, I believe, that relationship building IS part of your job. So although you may be inclined to feel that you wasted 30 minutes to an hour talking, it is often an investment that can pay large dividends in the future, both for you and the staff member involved.

On the other hand, if as a psychologist, you remain cemented to your own work area and never circulate within the institution, your view of the institution becomes stilted and others view of you also becomes inaccurate. In moving about, you can learn about the various activities and responsibilities that other staff are involved with, thus deepening your appreciation of the role they play. It is interesting to me that the more I come to learn about other staff's responsibilities, the more I seem to appreciate them and the more they seem to appreciate my role, as well.

Going one step further beyond this is to actually spend time working in the position of other staff members. I have been quite fortunate in the institution in which I work to be given the opportunity to temporarily fill in for correctional officers when situations arise in which the custodial staff is understaffed. This has placed me in the position of supervising a housing unit full of inmates, being responsible for coordinating inmate movement within the institution and supervising the overall compound, driving a perimeter patrol vehicle armed with a variety of firearms to prevent escapes and escape attempts, and controlling access of individuals in and out of controlled housing units occupied by maximum security inmates and disciplinary problems. Initially, such duty is somewhat foreboding, but the experience is priceless. It gives you firsthand experience in the day-to-day operations of the institution and direct experience with the duties of the frontline correctional officers. This is a wonderful educational opportunity that can greatly enhance your understanding of the functioning of the institution as a whole and help you understand in other instances explanations of both employee and inmate behavior. You will understand when an inmate describes a problem that they had with a particular officer because you know that officer and you know what responsibilities he has in the post he occupies because you have worked it yourself. Obviously, this can also cut down on inmates' ability to manipulate you about the various processes and procedures they claim to be subjected to or to help them understand in delicate situations that an officer who they feel mistreated by was actually performing his or her assigned functions which they may not have understood.

This is, without a doubt, one of the quickest and easiest methods for developing an appreciation of what other employees do in the institution while earning you great respect from other employees for your willingness to perform such duties, while recognizing their importance and respecting the job that you temporarily occupy. This further prevents you from being classified as an overpaid, self-important, doctor that has little idea or concern of what actually is going on in the institution around you.

I have talked to many psychologists who think I am somewhat deviant in my appreciation for such assignments and willingness to engage in them. Many of my colleagues outright refuse to engage in such activities or resist as much as they possibly can. The excuse most often heard is that operating in a correctional officers role is at odds with being a psychologist who engenders inmates to trust them and serves as a repository of confidential information about them, or that operating in this role will interfere with the therapeutic relationship or potentially place the psychologist in an ethical dilemma of whether to act as an officer or psychologist in a given situation. The truth of the matter is, I believe, they are responding to their own inner fears that naturally occur whenever someone is given a new task to complete that they are unfamiliar with, made all the harder by the great degree of responsibility that accompanies any correctional post. In the end, they miss out on a great opportunity and learning experience. They also lose a great deal of respect from other staff who inevitably learn in one fashion or another of their stance. The result is a distancing and separation between the psychologists and much of the rest of the institutional staff, an outcome that inevitably makes one's job harder than it has to be.

The issue of keeping secrets that impact on security issues was discussed in an earlier chapter. If one is not maintaining secrets about inmates that are security-related, then there should be no substantial conflict of interest here. Does an inmate's trust in their psychologist vanish when the psychologist cuffs them while working a shift in the special housing unit? In my experience, inmates recognize their role as inmates and recognize that the psychologist is performing established procedure for the environment. I have never had a therapeutic relationship harmed by such activities. In fact, it has often put me in positions that allowed me to better understand the inmate involved by being able to observe them outside the office and to interact in a more informal manner with them that actually cemented any relationship, rather than harming it. I believe that most psychologists, once they overcome their initial anxieties about "working in the field" will come to see it as a unique and valuable learning experience.

CONCLUSION

As in any environment, working with co-workers can be as challenging as performing one's assigned tasks. In the correctional environment, though, making efforts to build appropriate relationships and be accepted by staff that usually possess a different perspective from the psychologist is an essential part of your job that can assist you in fulfilling many of your other responsibilities effectively. Although providing personal counseling services to your own co-workers can, at times, feel awkward or create undesired complications, being the treatment provider helps you control staff's perceptions of psychologists functions. Additionally, in many cases it can assist you in establishing strong appreciative relationships with key institutional staff.

Chapter 8

CONTEMPLATING A CAREER IN CORRECTIONAL PSYCHOLOGY

THERE ARE STRENGTHS AND WEAKNESSES of any decision we make and any workplace we select for ourselves. Whether working within the field of corrections as a psychologist is a viable or even enviable choice is a highly personal decision and there are no set of criteria one must have in order to find the field to be rewarding and fulfilling. However, I hope in the next few paragraphs to provide some insights as to qualities that one might wish to consider that in my experience, might be more likely to result in someone having a positive versus a negative experience in this particular line of work. It is hoped that in the very least the discussion will allow anyone considering entering the field to at least make a more informed decision about selecting a job that most of us possess little information about, not to mention the lack of validity of the information that one may often be basing a decision.

DEVELOPMENTAL CONSIDERATIONS: WORKING WITH THE ADOLESCENT MENTALITY

For someone considering work in this area without prior experience, I think it is helpful to look at how your professional (and perhaps non-professional) experiences have been in working with the adolescent population. The reason for this is that regardless of whether you work with inmates who are twelve years old or seventy years old you will find that in many respects, you will be dealing with individuals who function at the adolescent stage of development. If this is a stage that has given you few opportunities for success and enjoyment in the past, you are probably wise to avoid entering this area of work. If, on the other hand, working with those devious adolescent children with their traumatic crises has been a source of challenge and self-fulfillment, you may be on the right track.

As detailed in the earlier chapter on inmates, many of them seem oddly out of place in discussing issues more typically encountered in the adolescent years. Whatever problems or processes that prevented them from more fully developing into the mature adult stages of cognitive, identity and moral development often seem to remain active during their incarceration. Some adolescent defiance, ego-centrism, and cemented convictions of their own cause can be difficult to deal with in a budding adult. Dealing with virtually the same issues and behaviors in a forty-year-old man can stretch the limitations of anyone's patience.

PSYCHOLOGICAL DEVELOPMENT OF PRISON INMATES

Moral Development

As an example of the rigidity with which many offenders remain entrenched at adolescent (or even preadolescent) stages of development, consider how Kohlberg's (1976 1979) theory of moral development applies to most prison inmates. Typically as children mature, they pass from what Kohlberg termed the preconventional to conventional level of moral development in late childhood to early adolescence. As a result, most adolescents and adults reason at Kohlberg's stage 4 or 5 which simply means that the individual becomes capable of looking beyond personal consequences and able to consider others perspectives. Conventional morality thus focuses on upholding the rules of society. At the preconventional level, however, societal rules are respected only to the extent that it falls within the individual's immediate self-interest. As research has shown (Jennings, Kilkenney, & Kohlberg, 1983) and clinical experience will confirm repetitively, most inmates have never progressed beyond preconventional morality. Interestingly enough, this does not seem to occur because of an inability to rationalize their decisions in the more advanced manner or to other intellectual limitations. I have encountered numerous inmates who are quite aware of how others perceive the situations they encounter, including understanding others' moral objections to their behaviors and decisions. However well they may understand these conventional level points of view, it appears some sort of hedonistic personality glitch or contemptual feelings towards societal mores causes an override of standard decision-making to occur and criminal behavior to take place. The other interesting tendency is for many inmates to be able to express conventional mores to a therapist while incarcerated only to return to their previous behavior upon release. Thus, an inmate may unequivocally state that they have "seen the light" and will never return to criminal acts again because they care too much about hurting their parents, spouses, and children. However, when released from confinement the value of these relationships, particularly when they do not provide full and immediate satisfaction of the inmates desires, diminishes considerably and quickly. This is not altogether different from the severe drug or alcohol abuser who repeatedly is able to evoke assistance from family and friends on promises of true reform with no intention of actually giving up their drug of choice. Probably a good example of this type of moral reasoning can be taken from an example discussed earlier in the book of an inmate who was accepting of his wife and their son living with a "wealthy" gentleman for whom she provided sexual favors as long as she sent him money in prison to spend on snack foods.

The clear majority of studies in the research literature show a correlation between relatively high moral judgment and what is commonly considered to be moral behavior, which includes such things as honesty, resistance to temptation and altruism (Kohlberg & Candee, 1984). Additionally, there is some evidence that moral development can be advanced in prison inmates within a correctional environment. Wiley (1987) demonstrated advances in moral growth of inmates enrolled in standard education classes when exposed to andragogical (as opposed to pedagogical) teaching styles. This suggests the possibility that interventions in this area might be effective and useful in altering the antisocial behaviors of some inmates. More formal training efforts have also shown an ability to advance the measured moral reasoning of inmates (Arbuthnot, 1984), but the question of whether the inmates will then choose to engage in greater degrees of moral behavior following such intervention remains unanswered.

Cognitive Development

Other cognitive "difficulties" commonly encountered among inmates, characteristic of the adolescent or preadolescent state, include the ability to engage in hypothetical-deductive reasoning, which is characterized by a more flexible cognitive style in which one becomes capable of considering a number of alternatives to a problem, weighing them, and then selecting the one most conducive to success. Instead, with inmates, you find they will often come to impulsive decisions based on preconventional moral reasoning about how to solve their problems and become so fixated with that as the solution as to be disinterested in seriously considering alternative ideas. In the prison environment this often involves decisions on how to handle difficulties with interpersonal relationships with those on the outside. In such situations some inmates can be helped through this process (often with much effort on the therapists part) to recognize that their initial ideas on how to most successfully manage their situation are not, in fact, their best available alternative. While such successes can be momentarily satisfying from the therapist's standpoint, it is unfortunate that our advice is often only utilized when we can convince the inmate of the best choice of behavior using preconventional forms of logic ourselves.

While this may be disconcerting to some degree, it also points out an often effective means of dealing with inmates involved in crisis situations (engaging in rule violating behaviors, or threats to self/others). It is probably unwise to appeal to many of them in anything but preconventional logic. That is, if you want to convince them to stop doing something, you must somehow convince them that it is to their direct benefit in the long run. To appeal to other, higher level, reasons is probably under-productive at best and inflammatory at worst. An example would be to appeal to an inmate in regards to how their behavior may affect their children, parents, etc. Such as appeal may well be reacted to with a litany of ways these family members have "failed" to demonstrate their love and further inflame the inmates depressive or agitated state.

I am familiar with one psychologist who routinely utilizes a technique of trying to convince inmates who are acting out how "immature" and "childish" their behavior is. When this psychologist (of generally dubious abilities) moved to a high security environment, his technique quickly served as a way of inflating situations or even creating them anew after incidents had settled down. He quickly became disliked by both inmates and staff alike at least partly from this inability to meet inmates at a cognitive and moral level they could identify with (and thereby demonstrating the attainment of only preconventional logic himself).

Adolescents also tend to develop the capacity to "think about their own thinking," and therefore to consider the development of their own concepts and ideas. Inmates typically do not possess this ability to any reasonable degree as demonstrated by their significant lack of psychological insight into their own motivations for their choices and behavior. Once again, this is a skill that can be worked on and developed within a therapeutic relationship, but most inmates lack the requisite motivation to affect significant personality change. On the contrary, their own narcissism prevents the consideration of altering their current patterns.

Finally, the more naive cognitive style of the inmate often demonstrates the cognitive deficits of the early adolescent in the prevalence of adolescent egocentricism and a belief in the personal fable. The first leads them to have difficulty differentiating between what they and others are thinking, leading them to believe that others would behave just as they do if not for their greater "fear" of punishment and an inability to comprehend others' reasons for preventing them from following through on what they have reasoned to be the best course of action. The personal fable involves the belief that what they are feeling is original, new and somehow unique to them. Thus, you will hear an inmate profess that "they" don't belong here. I have heard inmates lament that although they admit to having committed several crimes for which they are convicted, they do not consider themselves to be "criminals," and do not belong in prison.

UNIQUE CONSIDERATIONS OF WORKING IN CORRECTIONS

Another hallmark of the inmate, as well as the adolescent, is a lack of due respect for authority. If one desires or requires to work in an environment in which you are given due respect for your position and status in life, the correctional environment is less than satisfying. Inmates, as well as staff, respond better to a down-to-earth approach from those that do not try to place themselves on a pedestal due to education or career position. One cannot expect in the correctional environment to be immediately accepted as a resident authority on behavior and interpersonal relations, instead you must earn this respect from both staff and inmates. You can expect and should be able to handle being subjected to verbal abuse involving profanity that will be made as direct as possible against you. Of course, such behavior is a symptom in those we are dealing with and needs to be accepted in our own minds as nothing more than an immature response to the frustration and fear that the person speaking is desperately trying to manage in the only way they know how. It is necessary that you not only understand this last statement, but can truly believe it. If inmates see that you take such abuse to heart to any degree whatsoever, the abuse will only be increased to ever higher levels and fine-tuned to just the spot that seems to hurt you the most.

It becomes necessary to have a positive and mature sense of self when you begin so that verbal abuse is not taken to heart. Additionally, you should be able to provide sufficient reinforcement for your efforts as a person and as a psychologist to not be overly reliant on external reinforcement from others. Relative to most other mental health care environments, this is not a place full of "warm fuzzies." Emotions other than anger and frustration are not plentiful in their display in the correctional arena. This goes not only for inmates, but staff as well. As outlined above, one needs to build up a shield to some degree to avoid being hurt. The shield also prevents one from being targeted for manipulation and perhaps threats in that you should avoid revealing much in the way of personal information to inmates. Inmates are never your friends, only your clients. To reveal too much of yourself leaves you vulnerable. While this is the safe way to proceed, it can appear to leave the environment in which you work somewhat barren and uninviting.

One of the most difficult adjustments I had to make when moving into my office at a prison after working in the outside community was that I was no longer able to proudly display pictures of my loved ones. In past jobs it seemed that occasional glances at these pictures could be a source of comfort and reassurance on those difficult days that seemed to have no end. Looking at a desk devoid of personal possessions can almost make one feel out of place. The shield remains largely in place before co-workers as well because of the presence of inmates in virtually all parts of the institution. As a result, to expect positive feedback from other staff or inmates is to often be disappointed. Additionally, one cannot escape the feeling of potentially being set up when an inmate speaks too positively of you. As a result, the successful correctional psychologist, I believe, is one that can set goals to accomplish and strive to achieve them independently, allowing oneself to grant self-praise whenever it is deserved and be satisfied in your duties in the absence of public acknowledgment from others.

Institutions vary considerably in the manner in which they are run and in the degree to which their funding allows them to provide those things they should. Public desires to incarcerate criminals for an ever-increasing range of crimes and for ever-increasing lengths of time, accompanied by resistance to provide rehabilitative options and increased funding has led to increasing crowding and danger in many of our prisons nationwide. The degree of problems varies considerably depending upon the institutions management style, age, level of crowding, security level, staff training/education and degree of funding. In some states and counties, conditions are quite stark, with inadequate levels of staffing, serious overcrowding and inadequate screening of staff applicants. I would strongly recommend before committing oneself to working within any correctional institution the opportunity to meet as many staff members as possible, on personally observing the inmates and conditions in which they live, and getting to know the colleagues you will be working with. Red flags should obviously fly if a general chaos seems to exist within the institution, if staff appear uneducated and/or inexperienced and if colleagues are non-existent or lack professionalism.

When considering employment at a particular institution carefully assess the staffing levels before taking a job. Being the only psychologist at a large facility is a daunting task. Being one of only two psychologists places great importance on ensuring your co-worker is trustworthy, competent and industrious. My unfortunate experience is that these qualities cannot be assumed. Too often, corrections has served as a repository for psychologists that are unable to attain licensure to practice anywhere else and/or don't have the skills to do so. Further complicating this matter is that the shortage of psychologists and stressful nature of the job often doesn't prevent such psychologists from obtaining promotions largely due to their length of employment. Also, managerial staff that serve over the department often have little comprehension of what psychologists do and how. This allows relatively incompetent psychologists to contrive careers, at times, that fellow psychologists around them can become incredulous about. As correctional institutions are largely public agencies, politics, nepotism and manipulativeness are often major factors in determining promotions.

Before committing to a job, evaluate staff turnover in those that have come before you. How much turnover has there been and where did previous employees go? Were they promoted (positive) or did they leave the correctional field altogether (negative). If you gather their name, contact them and discuss their experiences directly. For staff that continue to be employed, ask to talk with each privately and get their impression of supervision, management and the institution as a whole. If this is discouraged, you probably need to move on. If allowed, but staff are clearly uncomfortable and less than straightforward, move on, but don't indicate why to protect them from possible reprisals.

If you are hoping to get supervision towards licensure in a job make sure you get a written commitment from the person who is going to provide it and ensure they are qualified to do so. If it is to be provided by someone other than who you are discussing employment with, meet with the supervisor directly and privately to ensure they are aware of the arrangement and committed to fulfilling it.

Although the necessity of being able to provide self-reinforcement to oneself without having to rely on others was emphasized above, working as the only psychologist within an institution can be a particularly difficult and lonely experience. This should be expected in situations where the psychologist is serving in a part-time consulting role, but a full-time position as the only mental health professional invites early burnout. Colleagues, if competent and respected, can be a great source of camaraderie and strength to get through your day. In difficult cases, the opportunity to gain an outside perspective is occasionally needed by all of us. On a day-to-day basis having someone to share your treatment triumphs, failures or merely amusing anecdotes can greatly eliminate the sense of isolation that could easily develop otherwise. To become too isolated by lack of collegial support in an environment that is emotionally cold and not always greatly appreciative of your presence by either staff or inmate, is to invite dissatisfaction, disillusionment and burnout.

It is probably more important for the correctional psychologist to have or develop outside interests than it is for psychologists working in other areas. After all, your patients are not as likely to open up new windows of opportunity in your day-to-day interactions with them unless you aspire to rob a bank at some point in your career. The constant exposure to descriptions of crime and engagement in criminal behavior can easily lead one to develop negative ideas about humanity. After all, Carl Rogers worked with college students, not inmates. Retaining a positive, humanistic, perspective can be challenging when you are only exposed to those who exemplify the worst elements of selfishness, greed, and violence within our society. This may be combated somewhat by exposure to staff members, but the overwhelming amount of your interpersonal interaction will probably be with inmates, not staff.

Without some balance in one's personal life to offset the dark side of human nature, it is easy to lose the ability to experience warmth, trust and empathy in relations with others. I am afraid the correctional field is littered with staff that possess hardened, sarcastic attitudes that have become more entrenched over their years of service. Good stress management skills, outside interests and interpersonal relationships are a must for continued success and survival. This may also be made more difficult by an environment that seems to foster staff members who neglect their physical and psychological health out of a denial of their own limitations, who often work long hours through personal commitment and who may suffer for the effects of their job commitment through intrafamilial conflict. In short, your non-professional colleagues may often have surprisingly atrocious stress management practices, such you will not be able to rely on them to be a positive influence if they come to compose a significant degree of your social group.

Finally, given the nature of this field, one should be physically and psychologically prepared for dealing with physical confrontations and crises. As a psychologist, you will not be excused entirely from fulfilling a law enforcement role on occasions. Though specific duties vary by system, in the Federal system all employees receive the same basic training for dealing with institutional crises and disturbances. Thus, when problems develop your role as a psychologist may be made secondary to your role as a correctional officer. One needs to understand

and accept this from the start. Additionally, you may be required to demonstrate basic levels of physical agility and strength commensurate with such responsibilities. Though requirements are likely to be minimal, they are nevertheless an important element of the job.

Among other practices that can help one to deal with the stresses of the correctional environment and prevent burnout over time is to maintain contact with other professionals in the field of psychology both within and outside the correctional arena. If you are fortunate enough to work in a setting with multiple psychologists, it is probably a wise practice to utilize their special expertise in matters you are less experienced in. It is also a good idea to call on them for second or even third opinions in more stressful cases, such as how to handle individuals who are threatening or have attempted self-harm. The presence of other professionals spreads not only the responsibility for decision making, but the stress that accompanies the tough calls as well. There are often cases in which a psychologist may wish to call an inmate on their manipulativeness and not take the safe and easy route of placing them on suicide watch, for example. However, shouldering the responsibility for such a courageous call, even when its right on the money, is much more difficult when that psychologist is taking full responsibility for the decision rather than being able to collaborate with another. The author is fully aware that some inmates are able to find the button in each of us that can come to cloud our judgment in making the best, most caring decisions, for them. Sometimes a psychologist is able to recognize that they have lost their professional distance, sometimes they are not. Having a colleague to call on when the stress starts to build and liability issues are at stake can help one make the right decisions in comfort and be able to go home without haunting thoughts keeping you awake at night.

Another strategy for maintaining ones sanity and preventing burnout is to fully recognize that your "patient population" did not come to you by choice. As such, many of them are not in the least interested in changing themselves. The best strategy is to make oneself available to all inmates, but in the absence of serious mental illness or clear psychological distress, leave the initial step of seeking help to them. By pushing oneself on someone who does not desire help you accomplish two things: (1) You push someone who needs your help and has difficulty trusting others farther away from you; (2) You create an enormous burden of accepting responsibility for someone elses bad choices, resulting in personal feelings of helplessness and, eventually, burnout. Let those who do not need or want your help be, do what is necessary for those who need it, but don't want it, and then try to make a difference for those who want your assistance, regardless of their need, for it is this last category of inmates that will obtain significant benefit from you and you will obtain some sense of accomplishment and satisfaction from. I have often been amazed at how some psychologists can become so frustrated trying to treat an inmate who has no interest in being treated. If an inmate does not want treatment and is creating no significant problem for himself or others, leave the door open, but let him be.

In talking to psychologists in the field who have been in their work for a period of years and do not seem to have been to unduly effected by it, I have found some commonalities. They often have a small number of inmates that they have done long-term extensive therapy with. These inmates have not necessarily been the most needful of services, but have served as a conduit to allow the psychologist to practice their best clinical skills on a cooperative subject to keep those skills from stagnating and dying. That is not to say that the inmates involved did not benefit, because they usually did. However, the length and depth of the relationship may have often been as significant in what they received as were any techniques or advice they may have received from the psychologist.

Experienced psychologists usually have developed an area of specialization or expertise within the area that they have kept active in. For some it has been hostage negotiation, for some anger management, for others meditation, and so on. The important thing is that one applies ones strengths and interests to the environment, rather than halfheartedly responding to what the environment seems to dictate. That's not to say that the psychologist can choose to totally ignore the treatment needs of the population they are charged with, but totally ignoring their own needs is likely to be just as dangerous. The limits of what types of interventions can be applied within this population are primarily dictated by the individual psychologists creativity. Most importantly, successful psychologists have interests outside the institution from which they can achieve fulfillment, stimulation and support.

OPPORTUNITIES FOR PERSONAL/CAREER DEVELOPMENT

Working as a psychologist in a correctional environment offers one a surprising array of variety in your occupational duties. In the Federal Prison System, for example, when psychologists are initially hired they are put through the same "basic training" as all other correctional staff members. This training is composed of three primary elements: academics, self-defense and firearms. The academic portion provides you with a basic understanding of the correctional system on an institutional and system-wide level and introduces you to the various policies and procedures used in the day-to-day operations of each facility. Included in this is training on such issues as constitutional law, understanding and managing inmates, requirements and procedures for use of force and emergency procedures. Self-defense classes introduce fundamental skills for use in handling physically aggressive inmates. Firearms training teaches the fundamentals of marksmanship and practice in the use of a variety of weapons. The training as a whole provides you with a good general background to assist in your understanding of all the various operations within the institution and seeks to engender a general level of cooperativeness and shared sense of purpose amongst all types of correctional service personnel. Although it may seem superfluous initially, the information learned helps one understand well the pressures and responsibilities faced by staff members in other departments and the knowledge helps you to best be able to fulfill your own unique role in the institution. Additionally, it prepares you with the requisite skills to fill virtually any post within the institution. It is easy to find a psychologist, giving to their educational level and knowledge of people, in the role of filling in for Associate and Assistant Wardens, or even the Warden themselves. As mentioned in other chapters, it is possible, even sometimes necessary, to be assigned to work in the role of a front-line correctional officer in some institutions. While I have heard some of my colleagues gripe about such responsibilities and many outright refuse, my experience has been nothing but positive. From the standpoint of the current discussion, accepting temporary duty assignments of this nature for a few hours or a day allows you to experience both the institution and the inmates from a different perspective, one that can sometimes be quite enlightening. I have never finished this type of duty without having both an increased understanding of the institution and the officers that work within it as well as a deepened sense of respect for them. From an entirely personal point of view, it gives one the chance to shed the usual duties of a psychologist and to "put on a different hat" for a while. The variety and intellectual stimulation that this causes can help to fight symptoms of boredom and burnout, by escaping the day-to-day drudgery of any job that becomes to predictable and monotonous.

Besides cross-training in correctional work, most prison systems also offer a variety of opportunities within the realm of psychology itself. There is usually the freedom to develop your own programs to offer to staff members and inmates, with common topics covering areas such as stress management, communication skills, relapse prevention, release preparation, pain management, veterans groups and anger control. This is an area where one's own expertise or interests can be allowed to flourish to the benefit of the institution and yourself as you will not only be involved in the group itself, but come into contact with individuals who possess treatment needs in areas of your professional interest that may be further pursued by mutual consent. In addition, specialty programs available in many state and federal agencies are typically directed by psychologists. These include forensic study programs, inpatient psychiatric treatment programs for the incarcerated mentally ill, drug treatment programs, and treatment for sexual offenders. Psychologists are usually asked to play a central role in being a member of hostage negotiation teams and as providers of debriefing sessions and therapy for staff and their families involved in institutional crises.

Psychologists in the correctional setting are also commonly involved in administrative issues of their institution, providing further opportunities to develop one's personal interests and provide psychology's unique perspective to the developing field of corrections. Some psychologists exposed to this aspect of the job have found themselves becoming increasingly enamored and involved with it to the point of "jumping ship" from the specific domain of psychology to pursue other avenues of career and personal development. There are numerous examples of associate wardens and wardens who have followed this path from psychologist to institutional administrator. In fact, a recent Director of the Federal Bureau of Prisons, Kathleen Sawyer, was herself a psychologist who rose through the ranks of that system. Short of totally altering ones career path, there are numerous opportunities to participate in training that further develops one's knowledge of many different aspects of this multifaceted domain.

THEORETICAL CONSIDERATIONS

The increasing emphasis on managed care and limitations of insurance coverage generally have altered the delivery of psychology-service delivery to an increasing prevalence of short-term therapies. While one may think of prisons that are occupied by long-term inmates as a last bastion to provide long-term insight-oriented treatment, this is not often the case. As outlined in Chapter 3 on the responsibilities of correctional psychologists, one's tasks in this environment are multifaceted. As you are also operating within a public service environment (read bureaucracy) there exists substantial documentation requirements (read paperwork). The limitations on one's time and the unpredictability of many of the most time-consuming crises, make the establishment of long-term commitments to individual therapy very difficult. As one may be responsible for the psychological evaluation and health maintenance of hundreds of inmates on an ongoing basis, patchwork treatment in times of crisis or other unusual need is typically sufficient to fill one's workday. Additionally, the population you are involved with tends to be quite concrete in their thinking and less prone to want to investigate the early developmental underpinnings of their current behavior. Insight may be nice, but what they really need are tools to control their impulsivity and anger and increase their acceptance of traditional societal values. You will probably find few inmates willing to engage in long-term intensive personal investigation. You will find still fewer that are able to comprehend the significance of personal insights achieved through such endeavors. That is not to question their overall intelligence, but there tends to be substantial naivete regarding psychological matters, even among the more intelligent inmate population. A psychologist's pursuit of more intensively focused individual therapy with a specific inmate is likely governed more to fulfilling the psychologists personal need than that of the inmate.

In dealing with inmates, there is an almost everpresent existence of externalizing and narcissistic tendencies, neither of which are conducive to therapies designed to explore the individual's personal contribution to their life problems. As a psychologist, it may be interesting to ponder psychodynamic explanations of the origins of behavior we witness, but our interventions must necessarily remain focused on clear, concrete and present-oriented solutions. This applies to staff interventions and our explanations of inmates to staff members as well. Law enforcement personnel are likely to interpret psychodynamic interpretations as psychobabble and to an extent they are correct. As one example, consider a study by Schultz-Ross (1993) hypothesizing that those employed in correctional facilities may have unconscious feelings of a desire or need for punishment. While perhaps an interesting anecdotal hypothesis for those of a certain theoretical persuasion, such suggestions do not help endear our profession to the larger correctional field. Psychodynamic explanations of inmate behaviors serve no pragmatic purpose. They accomplish nothing in the way of inmate management or security maintenance and serve only to solidify correctional staff's perception of the psychologist as providing little useful purpose to the organization's cause. Instead, as with inmate interactions, explanations and interpretations of inmates behaviors and suggestions for their proper management should also be concrete, clear and present-oriented. Psychologists with a pragmatic, problem-solving style will feel comfortable in a prison environment and be appreciated for their input. Psychoanalytically-minded professionals will likely find themselves isolated and unappreciated and dissatisfied with this field of endeavor.

CONCLUSION

The field of correctional psychology has been steadily increasing in recent years due to increases in prison populations and a growing appreciation for the contributions psychologists have to offer. Never before have psychologist-led drug treatment programs been so prevalent in our nation's prisons and never before have courts relied extensively on psychologists as expert witnesses in criminal cases where defendants mental status is an issue. This is a growing field that will provide many unique opportunities in the years to come for those interested in working in the field. Clearly, though, it is not meant for all. Mature-minded straightforward psychologists with down-to-earth conceptualizations of behavior with a strong sense of self-identity that will allow them to provide self-reinforcement in a less than blissful environment can find success and satisfaction in this area. An acceptance of the unique dangers, both physical and psychological, inherent in such a position is necessary. But if one is willing to practice good

stress management principles, maintain nourishing outside relationships and activities, such problems can usually be overcome.

REFERENCES

Advisory Council on First Aid and Safety. (2006). *ACFAS Scientific review of critical incident stress debriefing (CISD)*. Washington, D.C.: American Red Cross.

Albert, S., Fox, H., & Kahn, M. (1980). Faking psychosis on the Rorschach: Can expert judges detect malingering? *Journal of Personality Assessment, 44*, 115--119.

American Psychiatric Association. (1994). *Diagnostic and Statistical Manual of Mental Disorders* (4th ed). Washington, DC: American Psychiatric Association.

Anderson, E.W., Trethowan, W.H., & Kenna, J.C. (1956). An experimental approach to the problem of simulation in mental disorder. *Proceeding of the Royal Society of Medicine, 49*, 513–520.

Andrews, D.A., Bonta, J., & Hoge, R.D. (1990). Classification for effective rehabilitation: Rediscovering psychology. *CriminalJustice and Behavior, 17(1)*, 19–52.

Andrews, D.A., & Friesen, W. (1987). Assessments of anticriminal plans and the prediction of criminal futures: A research note. *Criminal Justice and Behavior, 14*, 33–37.

Andrews, D.A., & Kiessling, J.J. (1980). Program structure and effective correctionalpractices: A summary of the CaVIC research. In R.R. Ross & P. Gendreau (Eds.), *Effective Correctional Treatment*. Toronto: Butterworths.

Andrews, D.A., Zinger, I., Hoge, R.D., Bonta, J., Gendreau, P., & Cullen, F.T. (1990). Does correctional treatment work? A clinically relevant and psychologically informed meta-analysis. *Criminology, 28(3)*, 369–404.

Arbisi, P.A., & Ben-Porath, Y.S. (1995). An MMPI-2 infrequent response scale for use with psychopathological populations: The F(p) scale. *Psychological Assessment, 7*, 424–431.

Arbuthnot, J. (1984). Moral reasoning development programmes in prison: Cognitive developmental and critical reasoning approaches. *Journal of Moral Education, 13(2)*, 112–123.

Atkinson, L. (1986). The comparative validities of the Rorschach and the MMPI:A meta-analysis. *Canadian Psychology, 27*, 238–247.

Bagby, R.M., Buis, T.E., & Nicholson, R.A. (1995). Relative effectiveness of the standard validity scales in detecting fake-bad and fake-good responding: Replication and extension. Psychological Assessment, 7, 84–92.

Bagby, R.M., Rogers, R., Buis, T., Nicholson, R.A., Cameron, S.L., Rector, N.A., Schuller, D.R., & Seeman, M.V. (1997). Detecting feigned depression and schizophrenia on the MMPI-2. *Journal of Personality Assessment, 68(3)*, 650–664.

171

Baird, S.C., Heinz, R.C., & Bemus, B.J. (1979). *Project report 14: A two-year follow-up.* Wisconsin: Department of Health and Social Services, Case Classification/Staff Deployment Project, Bureau of Community Corrections.

Bash, I.Y., & Alpert, M. (1980). The determination of malingering. *Annals of the New York Academy of Sciences, 347*, 86–99.

Baskin, D.R., Sommers, I., & Steadman, H.J. (1991). Assessing the impact of psychiatric impairment on prison violence. *Journal of Criminal Justice, 19*, 271–280.

Baumeister, R.F., Smart, L, & Boden, J.M. (1996). Relation of threatened egotism toviolence and aggression: The dark side of high self-esteem. *Psychological Review, 103*, 5–33.

Benton, A.L. (1945). Rorschach performances of suspected malingerers. *Journal of Abnormal and Social Psychology, 40*, 94–96.

Berry, D.T.R., Baer, R.A., & Harris, M.J. (1991). Detection of malingering on the MMPI: A meta-analysis. *Clinical Psychology Review, 11*, 585–598.

Blader, J.C., & Marshall, W.L. (1989). Is assessment of sexual arousal worthwhile? A critique of current methods and the development of a response compatibility approach. *Clinical Psychology Review, 9*, 569–587.

Blau, T.H. (1994). *Psychological services for law enforcement.* New York: Wiley & Sons, Inc.

Bohn, M.J., Jr. (1979). Management classification for young adult inmates. *Federal Probation, 43(4)*, 53–59.

Bowen Jr., D.N. (1985). Personality and demographic characteristics of road deputies and correctional officers. *Dissertation Abstracts International, 45(II-B)*, 3605.

Bradford, J.M.W. (1990). The antiandrogen and hormonal treatments of sexual offenders. In W.L. Marshall, D.P. Law, & H.F. Barbaree's (Eds.), *Handbook of sexual assault: Issues, theories, and treatment of the offender* (pp. 297–310). New York: Plenum.

Brodsky, S.L. (1991). *Testifying in court: guidelines and maxims for the expert witness.* Washington, D.C.: American Psychological Association.

Brown, R.S., & Courtis, R.W. (1977). The castration alternative. *Canadian Journal of Criminology and Corrections, 19*, 196–205.

Bureau of Justice Statistics. (1993). *Survey of State prison inmates, 1991* (NCJ-136949). Washington, D.C.: U.S. Department of Justice.

Bureau of Justice Statistics. (1994). *Comparing federal and state prison inmates, 1991* (NCJ- 145864). Washington, D.C.: U.S. Department of Justice.

Bureau of Justice Statistics. (1995). *Drugs and crime facts, 1994* (NCJ-154043). Washington, D.C.: U.S. Department of Justice.

Bureau of Justice Statistics. (1996). *Prisoners in 1995* (NCJ-163916). Washington, D.C.: U.S. Department of Justice.

Bureau of Justice Statistics. (2005). *Suicide and homicide in state prisons and local jails* (August; NCJ-210036). Washington, D.C.: U.S. Department of Justice.

Bureau of Justice Statistics. (2006). *Prison and jail inmates at midyear 2005* (NCJ-213133). Washington, D.C.: U.S. Department of Justice.

Bureau of Justice Statistics. (2006b). *Mental health problems of prison and jail inmates* (NCJ-213600). Washington, D.C.: U.S. Department of Justice.

Bureau of Justice Statistics. (2007). *Prisoners in 2006* (NCJ-219416). Washington, D.C.: U.S. Department of Justice.

Burns, J.C., & Vito, G.F. (1994). An impact analysis of the Alabama boot camp program. *Federal Probation, 59(1),* 63–67.

Butcher, J.N., Dahlstrom, W.G., Graham, J.F., Tellegen, A.M., & Kaemmer, B. (1989). *MMPI- 2: Manual for administration and scoring.* Minneapolis, MN: University of Minnesota Press.

Butterfield, F. (2004). *Rise in killings spurs new steps to fight gangs.* New York Times, January 17.

Camp, C.G., & Camp, G.M. (1992). *Corrections Yearbook, 1992: Adult Corrections.* South Salem, NY: Criminal Justice Institute, Inc.

Camp, C.G., & Camp, G.M. (1995). *Corrections Yearbook, 1995: Adult Corrections.* South Salem, NY: Criminal Justice Institute, Inc.

Camp, C.G., & Camp, G.M. (2001). *The 2000 Corrections Yearbook: Adult corrections.* Middletown, CT: Criminal Justice Institute, Inc.

Carey, R.J., Garske, J.P., & Ginsberg, J. (1986). The prediction of adjustment to prison by means of an MMPI-based classification system. *Criminal Justice and Behavior, 13 4),* 347–365.

Chance, E.W., Bibens, R.F., Cowley, J., & Pouretedal, M. (1990). Lifeline: A drug/alcohol treatment program for negatively addicted inmates. *Journal of Reality Therapy, 9(2),* 33–38.

Cheek, F.E. (1984). *Stress management for correctional officers and their families.* College Park, Maryland: American Correctional Association.

Cheek, F.E., & Miller, M.D.S. (1983). The experience of stress for correctional officers: A double-bind theory of correctional stress. *Journal of Criminal Justice, 11,* 105–120.

Cooper, A.J. (1987). Sadistic homosexual pedophilia treatment with cyproterone acetate. *Canadian Journal of Psychiatry, 32,* 738–740.

Corbett Jr., R.P., & Petersilia, J. (1994). Up to speed: A review of research for practitioners. *Federal Probation, 58(2),* 60–66.

Cornelius, G.F. (1994). *Stressed out: Strategies for living and working in corrections.* Baltimore, MD: United Book Press.

Correia, K.M. (2000). Suicide assessment in a prison environment: A proposed protocol. *Journal of Criminal Justice and Behavior, 27(5),* 581–599.

Crowley, M.E. (1952). The use of the Kent EGY for the detection of malingering. *Journal of Clinical Psychology, 8,* 332–337.

Dahlstrom, W.G., Panton, J.H., Bain, K.P., & Dahlstrom, L.E. (1986). Utility of the Megargee-Bohn MMPI typological assignments: Study with a sample of death row inmates. *Criminal Justice and Behavior, 13,* 5–17.

Daniel, A.E., Robins, A.J., Reid, J.C., & Wifley, D.E. (1988). Lifetime and six month prevalence of psychiatric disorders among sentenced female offenders. *Bulletin of the American Academy of Psychiatry and the Law, 16,* 333–342.

Dollard, M.F., & Winefield, A.H. (1995). Trait anxiety, work demand, social support and psychological distress in correctional officers. *Anxiety, Stress and Coping: An International Journal, 8(1),* 25–35.

Dumond, R.W., & Dumond, D.A. (2002). The treatment of sexual assault victims (pp. 67–88), In Hensley, C. (Ed.), *Prison Sex: practice and policy*. Boulder, CO: Lynne Rienner Publishers.

Exner, J.E. Jr. (1986). Some rorschach data comparing schizophrenics with border-line and schizotypal personality disorders. *Journal of Personality Assessment, 50(3)*, 455–471.

Exner, J.E. Jr. (1993). *The Rorschach: A comprehensive system* (Volume 1: Basic Foundations, 3rd ed.). New York: John Wiley & Sons.

Exner, J.E. Jr. (1991). The Rorschach: A comprehensive system (Volume 2: Current Research and Advanced Interpretation. New York: John Wiley & Sons.

Federal Bureau of Investigation. (1994). *Crime in the United States*, 1993. Washington, D.C.: U.S. Department of Justice.

Feldman, M.J., & Grayley, J. (1954). The effects of an experimental set to stimulate abnormality on group Rorschach performance. *Journal of Projective Techniques, 18*, 326–334.

Field, G. (1989). The effects of intensive treatment on reducing the criminal recidivism of addicted offenders. *Federal Probation, 53*(4), 51–56.

Freund, K. (1965). Diagnosing heterosexual pedophilia by means of a test for sexual interest. *Behaviour Research and Therapy, 3*, 229–234.

Freund, K., & Watson, R.J. (1991). Assessment of the sensitivity and specificity of a phallometric test: An update of phallometric diagnosis of pedophilia. *Psychological Assessment, 3*, 254–260.

Furst, G. (2006). Prison-based animal programs: A national survey. *The Prison Journal, 86*, 407–430.

Gacono, C.B., & Meloy, J.R. (1994). *The Rorschach assessment of aggressive and psychopathic personalities*. Hillsdale, NJ: Lawrence Erlbaum Associates.

Ganellen, Wasyliw, O.E., Haywood, T.W., & Grossman, L.S. (1996). Can psychosis be malingered on the Rorschach? An empirical study. *Journal of Personality Assessment, 66*, 65–80.

Gilliard, D.K., & Beck, A.J. (1998). *Prisoners in 1997.* Washington, D.C.: United States Department of Justice. (NCJ-170014).

Goebel, R.A. (1983). Detection of faking on the Halstead-Reitan neuropsychological test battery. *Journal of Clinical Psychology, 39*, 731–742.

Goldkamp, J.S., & Weiland, D. (1993). *Assessing the impact of Dade County's felony drug court.* Washington, D.C.: U.S. Department of Justice.

Goldstein, H. (1945). A malingering key for mental tests. *Psychological Bulletin, 42*, 215–255.

Gough, H.G. (1950). The F minus K dissimulation index for the MMPI. *Journal of Consulting Psychology, 14*, 408–413.

Gough, H.G. (1954). Some common misconceptions about neuroticism. *Journal of Consulting Psychology, 18*, 287–292.

Graham, J.R., Watts, D., & Timbrook, R.E. (1991). Detecting fake-good and fake-bad MMPI-2 profiles. *Journal of Personality Assessment, 57(2)*, 264–277.

Grisso, T. (1988). *Competency to stand trial evaluations: A manual for practice.* New York: Plenum Press.

Grossman, L.S., & Wasyliw, O.E. (1988). A psychometric study of stereotypes: Assessment of malingering in a criminal forensic group. *Journal of Personality Assessment, 52*, 549–563.

Guy, E., Platt, J.J., Zwerling, I., & Bullock, S. (1985). Mental health status of prisoners in an urban jail. *Criminal Justice and Behavior, 12*, 29–53.

Hall, G.C.N. (1990). Prediction of sexual aggression. *Clinical Psychology Review, 10*, 229–245.

Hare, R. (1980). A research scale for the assessment of psychopathy in criminal populations. *Personality and Individual Differences, 1*, 111–119.

Hare, R. (1986). Twenty years of experience with the Cleckley psychopath. In W.H. Reid, D. Dorr, J.I. Walker, & J.W. Bonner (Eds.), *Unmasking the psychopath.* New York: W.W. Norton.

Hare, R. (1991). *Manual for the Revised Psychopathy Checklist.* Toronto: Multihealth Systems.

Hare, R., Forth, A.E., & Strachan, K.E. (1992). Psychopathy and crime across the lifespan. In R. Dev Peters, R.J. McMahon, & V.L. Quinsey (Eds.), *Aggression and violence throughout the lifespan.* Newbury Park, CA: Sage.

Harkrader, T., Burke, T., & Owen, S. (2004). Pound puppies: The rehabilitative use of dogs in correctional facilities. *Corrections Today, 66(2)*, 60–74.

Harris, G.T., Rice, M.E., & Cormier, C.A. (1991). Psychopathy and violent recidivism. *Law and Human Behavior, 15*, 625–637.

Harris, G.T., Rice, M.E., & Cormier, C.A. (1994). Psychopaths: Is a therapeutic community therapeutic? *Therapeutic Communities, 15*, 283–299.

Hart, S.D., Kropp, P.R., & Hare, R.D. (1988). Performance of male psychopaths following conditional release from prison. *Journal of Consulting and Clinical Psychology, 56*, 237–232.

Hawk, G.L., & Cornell, D.G. (1989). MMPI profiles of malingerers diagnosed in pretrial forensic evaluations. *Journal of Clinical Psychology, 45(4)*, 673–678.

Hayes, T.J. (1993). Residential drug abuse treatment in the Federal Bureau of Prisons. *Journal of Drug Issues, 23(1)*, 61–73.

Heaton, R.K., Smith, H.H., Lehman, R.A., & Vogt, A.T. (1978). Prospects for faking believable deficits on neuropsychological testing. *Journal of Consulting and Clinical Psychology, 46*, 892–900.

Heim, N. (1981). Sexual behavior of castrated sex offenders. *Archives of Sexual Behavior, 10*, 11–19.

Hodgins, S., & Cote, G. (1990). Prevalence of mental disorders among penitentiary inmates in Quebec. *Canada" Mental Health, 38*, 1–4.

Holinger, P.C. (1987). Violent deaths in the United States. New York: Guilford Press.
Humphrey, D.H., & Dahlstrom, W.G. (1995). The impact of changing from the MMPI to the MMPI-2 on profile configurations. *Journal of Personality Assessment, 64*, 428–439.

Hunt, H.F. (1948). The effect of deliberate deception on MMPI performance. *Journal of Consulting Psychology, 12*, 396–402.

Hunt, W.A. (1946). The detection of malingering: A further study. *Naval Medical Bulletin, 46*, 249–254.

Hunt, H.F., & Older, HI (1943). Detection of malingering through psychometric tests. *Naval Medical Bulletin, 41*, 1318–1323.

Hutton, H.E., & Miner, M.H. (1995). The validation of the Megargee-Bohn typology in African American and Caucasian forensic psychiatric patients. *Criminal Justice and Behavior, 22(3)*, 233–245.

Hutton, H.E., Miner, M.H., Blades, J.R., & Langfeldt, V.C. (1992). Ethnic differences on the MMPI Overcontrolled-Hostility Scale. *Journal of Personality Assessment, 58(2)*, 260–268.

Hutton, H.E., Miner, M.H., & Langfeldt, V.C. (1993). The utility of the Megargee Bohn typology in a forensic psychiatric hospital. *Journal of Personality Assessment, 60(3)*, 572–587.

Inwald, R., Knatz, H., & Shusman, E. (1982). *The Inwald Personality Inventory Manual.* New York: Hilton Research.

Iverson, G.L., Franzen, M.D., & Hammond, J.A. (1995). Examination of inmates ability to malinger on the MMPI-2. *Psychological Assessment, 7(1)*, 118–121.

Jennings, W, Kilkenney, R., & Kohlberg, L. (1983). Moral development theory and practice for youthful and adult offenders. In W Lauffer & J. Day (Eds.), *Personality Theory, Moral Development and Criminal Behavior.* Lexington: Lexington Books.

Johnson, D.L., Simmons, J.G., & Gordon, B.C. (1983). Temporal consistency of the Meyer-Megargee inmate typology. *Criminal Justice and Behavior, 10*, 263–268.

Judicial Council of California. (2006). *California drug court cost analysis study.* San Francisco, CA.

Junker, G.,Beeler, A., & Bates, J. (2005). sing trained inmate observers for suicide watch in a federal correctional setting: A win-win situation. *Psychological Services, 2*, 20–27.

Kennedy, T.D. (1986). Trends in inmate classification: A status report of two computerized psychometric approaches. *Criminal Justice and Behavior, 13 (2)*, 165–184.

Kohlberg, L.A. (1976). Moral stages and moralization. In Likona (Ed.), *Moral development: Current theory and research.* New York: Holt, Rinehart & Winston.

Kohlberg, L.A. (1979). *The meaning and measurement of moral development.* Heinz Werner Memorial Lecture. Worcester, MA: Clark University Press.

Kohlberg, L., & Candee, D. (1984). Relationship of moral judgment to moral action. In W.M. Kurtines & Gewirtz (Eds.), *Morality, moral behavior and moral development.* New York: Wiley & Sons.

Kurtz, R.A. (1993). The vulnerability of the MMPI-2, M test and SIRS to two strategies of malingering psychosis in a forensic setting. *Dissertation Abstracts International, 54 (1-A)*, 129–130.

Lamb, D.G., Berry, D.T.R., Wetter, M.W., & Baer, R.A. (1994). Effects of two types of information on malingering on the MMPI-2: An analogue investigation. *Psychological Assessment, 6*, 8–13.

Lee, D.R. (1983). Pet therapy: Helping patients through troubled times. *California Veterinarian, 5*, 24–25.

Lester, D. (1987). Suicide and homicide in USA prisons. *Psychological Reports, 61*, 126.

Lester, D. (1987b). *The death penalty.* Springfield, IL: Thomas.

Levitt, E.E., & Gotts, E.E. (1995). *The clinical application of MMPI special scales* (2nd Ed.). Hillsdale, NJ: Lawrence Erlbaum Associates, Inc.

Linton, J.C. (1995). Acute stress management with public safety personnel: Opportunities for clinical training and pro bono community service. *Professional Psychology: Research and Practice, 16(6)*, 566–573.

Lutejn, F. (1990). The MCMI in the Netherlands: First findings. *Journal of Personality Disorders, 4*, 297–302.

MacKenzie, D.L. (1993). Boot camp prisons in 1993. *NIJJournal, 227*, 21–28.

Major, B.C. (1992). The relationship between recidivism, drug history and participation in drug treatment programs among state prison inmates in the Northern California Reception Center at San Quentin State Prison. *Dissertation Abstracts International, 53(7)*, 3759-B.

Malcolm, P.B., Andrews, D.A., & Quinsey, V.L. (1993). Discriminant and predictive validity of phallometrically measured sexual age and gender preferences. *Journal of Interpersonal Violence, 8(4)*, 486–501.

Maletzky, B.W. (1991). *Treating the sexual offender.* Newbury Park, CA: Sage.

Man, C.D., & Cronan, J.P. (2002). Forecasting sexual abuse in prison: The prison subculture of masculinity as a backdrop for "deliberate indifference." *Journal of Criminal Law and Criminology, 9(1-2)*, 127–186.

Marlatt, G.A., & Gordon, J.R. (Eds.) (1985). *Relapse prevention.* New York: Guilford Press.

Marques, J.K., & Nelson, C. (1992). The relapse prevention model: Can it work with sex offenders? In R. Dev Peters, RI McMahon, & V.L. Quinsey (Eds.), *Aggression and violence throughout the lifespan.* Newbury Park, CA: Sage.

Marshall, W.L., & Barbaree, H.E. (1990). Outcome of comprehensive cognitive-behavioral treatment programs. In W.L. Marshall, D.R. Laws, & H.E. Barbaree (Eds.), *Handbook of sexual assault: Issues, theories and treatment of the offender.* New York: Plenum.

Marshall, W.L., Jones, R., Ward, T., Johnston, P., & Barbaree, H.E. (1991). Treatment outcome with sex offenders. *Clinical Psychology Review, 11*, 465–485.

Martin, S.S., Butzin, C.A., Saum, C.A., & Inciardi, J.A. (1999). Three-year outcome of therapeutic community treatment for drug-involved offenders in Delaware: From prison to work release to aftercare. *The Prison Journal, 79*, 294–320.

McCann, J.T., & Dyer, F.J. (1996). *Forensic Assessment with the Millon Inventories.* New York: Guilford Press.

McNally, R.J., Bryant, R.A., & Ehlers, A. (2003). Does early psychological intervention promote recovery from posttraumatic stress? *Psychological Science in the Public Interest, 4(2)*, 45–79.

Megargee, E.I. (1984). A new classification system for criminal offenders: VI. Differences among the types on the Adjective Checklist. *Criminal Justice and Beha-vior, 11(3)*, 349-376.

Megargee, E.I., & Bohn, M.J. (1977). A new classification system for criminal offenders: IV. Empirically determined characteristics of the ten types. *Criminal Justice and Behavior, 4*, 149–210.

Megargee, E.I., & Bohn, M.J. (1979). *Classifying criminal offenders: A new system based on the MMPI.* Newbury Park, CA: Sage.

Megargee, E.I., Cook, P.E., & Mendelsohn, G.A. (1967). Development and validation of an MMPI scale of assaultiveness in overcontrolled individuals. *Journal of Abnormal Psychology, 72,* 519–528.

Meloy, J.R., Hansen, T.L., & Weiner, I.B. (1997). Authority of the Rorschach: Legal citations during the past 50 years. *Journal of Personality Assessment, 69,* 53–62.

Melton, G.B., Petrila, J., Poythress, N.G., & Slobogin, C. (1997). *Psychological evaluations for the courts: A handbook for mental health professionals and lawyers* (2nd ed.). New York: Guilford Press.

Millon, T. (1977). *Millon Clinical Multiaxial Inventory.* Minneapolis: National Computer Systems.

Millon, T. (1981). Disorders of Personality. DSM-III: Axis II. New York: Wiley & Sons. Millon, T. (1983). *Millon Clinical Multiaxial Inventory Manual* (3rd ed.). Minneapolis: National Computer Systems.

Millon, T. (1987). *Manual for the Millon Clinical Multiaxial Inventory-II (MCMI-II).* Min-neapolis: National Computer Systems.

Millon, T. (1994). *Millon Clinical Multiaxial Inventory-III (MCMI-III) Manual.* Minneapolis: National Computer Systems.

Mittman, B.L. (1983). Judges ability to diagnose schizophrenia on the Rorschach: The effect of malingering (Doctoral dissertation, Long Island University, 1983). *Dissertation Abstracts International, 44,* 1248B.

Moneymaker, J.M., & Strimple, E.O. (1991). Animals and inmates: A sharing companionship behind bars. *Journal of Offender Rehabilitation, 16 (3/4),* 133–152.

Nacci, P.L., & Kane, T.R. (1983). The incidence of sex and sexual aggression in federal prisons. *Federal Probation, 47(4),* 31–36.

Nacci, P.L., & Kane, T.R. (1984). Inmate sexual aggression: Some evolving propositions, empirical findings, and mitigating counter-forces. *Journal of Offender Counseling, Services and Rehabilitation, 9 (1/2),* 1-20.

Nacci, P.L., & Kane, T.R. (1984). Sex and sexual aggression in Federal prisons: Inmate involvement and employee impact. *Federal Probation, 48(1),* 46–53.

National Institute of Justice. (1994). *Drug use forecasting 1993 annual report on adult arrestees* (NCJ-147411). Washington D.C.: U.S. Department of Justice.

Netter, B.F.C., & Viglione, DJ. (1994). An empirical study of malingering schizophrenia on the Rorschach. *Journal of Personality Assessment, 62,* 45–57.

Nichols, D.S., & Greene, R.L. (1997). Dimensions of deception in personality assessment: The example of the MMPI-2. *Journal of Personality Assessment, 68(2),* 251–266.

Ochberg, F. (1980). What is happening to the hostages in Tehran? *Psychiatric Annals, 10,* 186–189.

O'Donnell, C.R., Lydgate, T., & Fo, W.S.O. (1971). The buddy system: Review and follow-up. *Child Behavior Therapy, 1,* 161–169.

Ogloff, J.R., Wong, S., & Greenwood, A. (1990). Treating criminal psychopaths in a therapeutic community program. *Behavioral Sciences and the Law, 8,* 181–190.

O'Leary, W.D. (1989). Custodial suicide: Evolving liability considerations. *Psychiatric Quarterly, 60(1),* 31–71.

Parker, K.C.H., Hanson, R.K., & Hunsley, J. (1988). MMPI, Rorschach, and WAIS: A meta-analytic comparison of reliability, stability and validity. *Psychological Bulletin, 103*, 367–373.

Perry, G.G., & Kinder, B.N. (1990). The susceptibility of the Rorschach to malingering: A critical review. *Journal of Personality Assessment, 54*, 47–57.

Piotrowski, C., & Keller, J.W. (1989). Psychological testing in outpatient mental health facilities: A national study. *Professional Psychology: Research and Practice, 20*, 423–425.

Piotrowski, C., & Lubin, B. (1989). Assessment practices of Division 38 practioners. *Health Psychologist, 11*, 1.

Piotrowski, C., & Lubin, B. (1990). Assessment practices of health psychologists: Survey of APA Division 38 clinicians. *Professional Psychology: Research and Practice, 21*, 99–106.

Pithers, W.D. (1990). Relapse prevention with sexual aggressors: A method for maintaining therapeutic gain and enhancing external supervision. In W.L. Marshall, D.R. Laws & H.E. Barbaree (Eds.), *Handbook of Sexual Assault: Issues, theories, and treatment of the offender* (pp. 297–310). New York: Plenum.

Pollaczek, P.P. (1952). A study of malingering on the CVS Abbreviated Intelligence Scale. *Journal of Clinical Psychology, 8*, 77–81.

Prendergast, W.E. (1991). *Treating sex offenders in correctional institutions and outpatient clinics: A guide to clinical practice.* New York: Haworth Press.

Quinsey, V.L., & Chaplin, T.C. (1988). Preventing faking in phallometric assessments of sexual preference. In R. Prentky & V.L. Quinsey (Eds.), *Human aggression: contemporary perspectives.* New York: Annals of the New York Academy of Science (Vol. 528).

Quinsey, V.L., Chaplin, T.C., & Carrigan, W.F. (1979). Sexual preferences among incestuous and nonincentuous child molesters. *Behavior Therapy, 10*, 562–565.

Rempel, M., Fox-Kralstein, D., Cissner, A., Cohen, R., Labriola, M., Farole, D., Bader, A., & Magnani, M. (2003). *Executive Summary: The New York state adult drug court evaluation: Policies, participants and impacts.* New York: Center for Court Innovation.

Rice, M.E. (1997). Violent offender research and implications for the criminal justice system. *American Psychologist, 52(4)*, 414–423.

Rice, M.E., Harris, G.T., & Cormier, C.A. (1992). An evaluation of a maximum security therapeutic community for psychopaths and other mentally disordered offenders. *Law and Human Behavior, 76(4)*, 399–412.

Rice, M.E., Harris, G.T., & Quinsey, V.L. (1990). A follow-up of rapists assessed in a maximum-security psychiatric facility. *Journal of Interpersonal Violence, 5*, 435–448.

Rice, M.E., Quinsey, V.L., & Harris, G.T. (1991). Sexual recidivism among child molesters released from a maximum security psychiatric institution. *Journal of Consulting and Clinical Psychology, 59*, 381–386.

Richburg, K.B., & Surdin, A. (2008). *Fiscal pressures lead some states to free inmates early.* Washington Post: May 5.

Rogers, R. (Ed). (1997). *Clinical assessment of malingering and deception* (2nd ed.). New York: Guilford Press.

Rogers, R., Bagby, R.M., & Chakraborty, D. (1993). Feigning schizophrenia disorders on the MMPI-2: Detection of coached simulators. *Journal of Personality Assessment, 60*, 215–226.

Roman, J., Townsend, W., & Bhati, A.S. (2003). *Recidivism rates for drug court graduates: Nationally based estimates, final report* (NCJ-210229). Washington, D.C.: U.S. Department of Justice.

Rorschach, H. (1921). *Psychodiagnostik.* Bern: Bircher (Transl. Hans Huber Verlag, 1942).

Rosenberg, S.J., & Feldberg, T.M. (1944). Rorschach characteristics of a group of malingerers. *Rorschach Research Exchange, 8*, 141–158.

Rouse, J.J. (1991). Evaluation research on prison-based drug treatment programs and some policy implications. *International Journal of the Addictions, 26(1)*, 29–44.

Schreden, DJ. (1986). *Malingering: use of a psychological test battery to detect two kinds of simulation.* Ann Arbor, MI: University Microfilms International.

Schreden, DJ. (1988). The use of psychological tests to identify malingered symptoms of mental disorder. *Clinical Psychology Review, 8*, 451–476.

Schreden, DJ, & Arkowitz, H. (1990). A psychological test battery to detect prison inmates who fake insanity or mental retardation. *Behavioral Sciences and the Law, 8(1)*, 75–84.

Schultz-Ross, R.A. (1993). The prisoner's prisoner: The theme of voluntary imprisonment in the staff of correctional facilities. *Bulletin of the American Academy of Psychiatry and the Law, 21(1)*, 101–106.

Seamons, D.T., Howell, R.J., Carlisle, A.L., & Roe, A.L. (1981). Rorschach simulation of mental illness and normality. *Journal of Personality Assessment, 45*, 130–135.

Sherman, D. (1996). *Preventing and managing riots and disturbances.* Laurel, MD: American Correctional Association.

Shusman, Inwald, R.E., & Landa, B. (1984). Correctional officer job performance as predicted by the IPI and MMPI: A validation and cross-validation study. *Criminal Justice and Behavior, 11*, 309–329.

Simmons, J.G., Johnson, D.L., Gouvier, W.D., & Muzyczka, M.J. (1981). The MyerMegargee inmate typology: Dynamic or unstable? *Criminal Justice and Behavior, 8*, 49–54.

Simonsen, E., & Mortensen, E.L. (1990). Difficulties in translation of personality scales. *Journal of Personality Disorders, 4*, 290–296.

Sivec, H.J., Hilsenroth, M.J., & Lynn, S.J. (1995). Impact of simulating borderline personality disorder on the MMPI-2: A cost-benefits model employing base rates. *Journal of Personality Assessment, 64*, 295–311.

Stafford, M.C., & Weisheit, R.A. (1988). Changing age patterns of United States male and female suicide rates, 1934-1983. *Suicide and Life Threatening Behavior, 18(2)*, 149–163.

Strentz, T. (1982). *The Stockholm Syndrome: Law enforcement policy and hostage behavior.* In F.M. Ochberg & D.A. Soskis (Eds.), Victims of Terrorism. Boulder, CO: Westview Press.

Struckman-Johnson, C., & Struckman-Johnson, D. (2000). Sexual coercion rates in seven Midwestern prisons for men. *Prison Journal, 80*, 379–390.

Sylvester, S.F., Reed, J.H., & Nelson, D.O. (1977). *Prison homicides.* New York: Spectrum Publications.

Teplin, L.A., & Swartz, J. (1989). Screening for severe mental disorder in jails. *Law and Human Behavior, 13,* 1–18.

Timbrook, R.E., Graham, J.R., Keiller, S.W., & Watts, D. (1993). Comparison of the Wiener-Harmon Subtle-Obvious scales and the standard validity scales in detecting valid and invalid MMPI-2 profiles. *Psychological Assessment, 5,* 53–61.

Toch, H. (1965). *Task force for institutional violence: 'Aggressive history profile and known reasons for violence against victims."* Unpublished manuscript, California Department of Corrections.

Tsushima, W.T., & Anderson, R.M. (1996). *Mastering expert testimony: A courtroom handbook for mental health professionals.* New York: Erlbaum.

United States Department of Justice. (2000). *Prison and jail inmates at midyear 1999* (NCJ-181643). Washington, D.C.: Author.

United States Department of Justice. (1998). Triad drug treatment evaluation six-month report: Executive summary. Washington, D.C.: Author.

United States Department of Justice. (1996). *Annual report: Suicide prevention program.* Washington, D.C.: Author.

United States Supreme Court. (1997). *Kansas vs. Hendricks.* Argued December 10, 1996. Decided June 23, 1997.

Voorhis, P.V. (1988). A cross classification of five offender typologies: Issues of construct and predictive validity. *Criminal Justice and Behavior, 15(1),* 109–124.

Wachspress, M., Berenberg, A.N., & Jacobson, A. (1953). Simulation of psychosis. *Psychiatric Quarterly, 27,* 463–473.

Walters, G.D. (1988). Assessing dissimulation and denial on the MMPI in a sample of maximum security, male inmates. *Journal of Personality Assessment, 52,* 465–474.

Wasyliw, O.E., Grossman, L.S., Haywood, T.W., & Cavanaugh, J.L. (1988). The detection of malingering in criminal forensic groups: MMPI validity scales. *Journal of Personality Assessment, 52,* 321–333.

Watkins, C.E. Jr. (1994). Do projective techniques get a "bum rap" from clinical psychology training directors? *Journal of Personality Assessment, 63,* 387–389.

Wechsler, D. (2008). *Manual for the Wechsler Adult Intelligence Scale* (4th ed). San Antonio: The Psychological Corporation.

Weed, N.C., Ben-Porath, Y.S., & Butcher, J.N. (1990). Failure of Wiener and Harmon Minnesota Multiphasic Personality Inventory (MMPI) subtle scales as personality descriptors and as validity indicators. *Psychological Assessment: A Journal of Consulting and Clinical Psychology, 2,* 281–285.

Weiner, D.N. (1948). Subtle and obvious keys for the MMPI. *Journal of Consulting Psychology, 12,* 164–170.

Weiner, I.B. (1997, March). *Forensic Assessment with the Rorschach.* Presented at symposium of the Rorschach Workshops in Atlanta, Ga.

Weiner, I.B. (1996). Some observations on the validity of the Rorschach inkblot method. *Psychological Assessment, 8(2),* 206–213.

Weiner, I.B. (1997). Current status of the Rorschach inkblot method. *Journal of Personality Assessment, 68,* 5–19.

Weiner, I.B., Exner, J.E. Jr., & Sciara, A. (1996). Is the Rorschach welcome in the courtroom? *Journal of Personality Assessment, 67*, 422–424.

Wetter, M.W., Baer, R.A., Berry, D.T.R., & Reynolds, S.K. (1994). The effect of symptom information on faking on the MMPI-2. *Assessment, 1*, 199–207.

Wetter, M.W., Baer, R.A., Berry, D.T.R., Robison, L.H., & Sumpter, J. (1993). MMPI2 profiles of motivated fakers given specific symptom information: A comparison to matched patients. *Psychological Assessment, 5*, 317–323.

Wexler, H.K., Melnick, G., Lowe, L., & Peters, J. (1999). 3-year reincarceration outcomes for amity in-prison therapeutic community and aftercare in California. *The Prison Journal, 79*, 321–336.

Wiley, U. (1987). The effect of teaching style on the development of moral judgement in prison inmates. *Dissertation Abstracts International, 47(12-A)*, 4270.

Wright, K.N. (1988). The relationship of risk, needs and personality classification systems and prison adjustment. *Criminal Justice and Behavior, 15(4)*, 454–471.

Wrobel, T.A., Calovini, P.K., & Martin, T.O. (1991). Application of the Megargee MMPI typology to a population of defendants referred for psychiatric evaluation. *Criminal Justice and Behavior, 18(4)*, 397–405.

Zager, L.D. (1988). The MMPI-based criminal classification system: A review, current status, and future directions. *Criminal Justice and Behavior, 15(1)*, 39–57.

Ziskin, J., & Faust, D. (2009). *Coping with psychiatric and psychological testimony* (5th ed.). New York: Oxford University Press.

AUTHOR INDEX

SUBJECT INDEX

A

Antisocial Personality Disorder, 37, 77,
78–84, 102–105, 121, 123–125
Assessing Malingering in interview, 102–106

B

Beck Depression Inventory, 115
Bender Gestalt Test, 129
Bipolar Disorder, 79
Boot Camps, 63–65
Borderline Personality Disorder, 37–38, 79,
162–165

C

Confidentiality, 24–30
notification of limitations, 27
of staff information, 28–29
Correctional Psychologist
establishing relationships with
correctional staff, 137–139, 151–152
media portrayals, 21
number working, 9
perceptions of inmates, 16
perceptions of outsiders, 3–4
perceptions of staff, 20, 129, 137–138,
140–143
prescription privileges, 51, 53
reactions from others, 3
role in criminal justice system, 9–10
role in personnel selection, 68–70
trends in profession, 9–10
unique aspects of working in corrections,
159–165
working correctional posts, 99, 152–153
Crisis Interventions, 47–49

D

Depression, 34–35
Drug courts, 13
Drug Treatment, 55–58
research on effectiveness, 57–58

E

Emergency situations, 71–73
Employee assistance programs, 139–143
debriefing, 71–73
Expert testimony, 54, 115–116, 118–119

F

Forensic evaluations, 54

G

Gangs
affiliated offender(s), 22
in prison, 19, 23
Group therapy, 50–51
Growth
of corrections, 7–8
of inmate population, 7

H

Hostgage negotiation, 70–71

I

Inmate(s)
behavioral management of, 21–22
building relationship with, 17–18, 24, 27,
95–97, 98–99

W

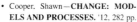

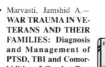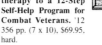

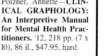